The Contemporary
Theatre, 1925

# The Contemporary Theatre, 1925

By James Agate

With an Introduction by
C. E. Montague

BENJAMIN BLOM  New York/London

TO
# IVOR BROWN

First Published 1926
Reissued 1969 by
Benjamin Blom, Inc., Bronx, New York 10452
and 56 Doughty Street, London, W.C. 1

Library of Congress Catalog Card Number 74-91407

Printed in the United States of America

# A Note of Admiration

## (1)

I LIKE to read every word of Mr. Agate's that I can get. He is one of the few dramatic critics who, from time to time, emit a veritable cry of delight. And that is not a thing to be missed. All great critical writing, so far as I can see, is the beautiful modulating of some cry of delight or other. Think of Lamb's descant upon Dicky Suett ; of Charlotte Brontë's on Rachel ; of Hazlitt's on Kean ; of Henry James's on Coquelin. It is the same with criticism of all the arts. Consider Mr. Ruskin's celebrated rhapsody on the first view of St. Mark's, and Pater's on the *Monna Lisa* ; what makes it impossible to read them without a surge of joyous exultation in oneself is that they breathe an impassioned delight ; you know for certain, while you read, that the writer was ravished above earth while he wrote ; the miracle had happened, and he felt like a man gazing into the glowing core of life itself.

Not many people ask a dramatic critic to be a critic. The rest bid him be "just" and "fair" and "judicial" ; purge the stage of abuses ; wave the ideal banner high, or else have common sense and fortify the crowd and the box-office in their simple faith that they are the men and that wisdom will die with them. It is as if the critic were a magistrate or a referee, an examiner or a rat-catcher. And some actors frankly want him to be a volunteer publicity agent, to saddle his modest Dapple and spur forth in the train of the several Don Quixotes of their own darling dreams.

A critic may serve one or more of these laudable ends. But only by the way. None of them is his main business. So far as he has any worth he is an artist himself, not an attendant on artists, nor an officer of justice, nor an expert in mensuration. His chief difference from other artists is that he tries to express in his art his personal emotion in presence of something seen and heard in a theatre, while they express their emotion in presence of something seen or heard outside it, or perhaps not seen or heard at all, but read in a book of yarns about Boadicea's whipping and Alfred's burnt cakes. It is more to the purpose that a critic should have vivacity and humour, atmosphere and gusto, as Mr. Agate has, than that he should practise ideal distributive justice in dishing out butter or beans to members of large casts. When Turner drew Twickenham for his *Liber Studiorum*, he left out some of the chief features of the place and threw in some of those of the neighbouring parish of Isleworth, and a very fine drawing he made by these means. And if any one should tell me—as no one has yet done—that Mr. Agate does not always allot exactly the right relative numbers of marks to the various actors who come before him to be written about, I shall rejoice in this new evidence of his wise exercise of the artist's right to select and emphasise, to pick freely from the material at hand, to pull about that which he takes, and to practise the divine inequity of Shakespeare's choice of heroes and heroines for commemoration.

This doctrine may give scandal to some actors. It revolts them to find a contumacious fellow picking out from their admirable performances just as much as he wants to set him going in his own little effort to achieve a beautiful vividness of self-expression. But in the end the great actor comes off pretty well at the hands of the artist-critic. Had ever actors such monuments as Fielding set up to Garrick, and as Lamb, the head of the whole artist-critic tribe, erected to the shades of Elliston and Munden? It may not be very certain to whom, in the hierarchy of merit, the monuments will go. But, at any rate, every one acting has a ticket in a lottery of some grandeur. He never knows when he may touch the spring of delight in some critic of genius. No doubt everything felt pretty much the same as usual to Rachel on the night when a shy, fiery-eyed, little school-marm, who was to make her immortal, strayed into the house.

(2)

"What!" I can almost hear somebody thinking indignantly to himself, "Is there, then, to be no objective standard of excellence? Is not a critic's first duty the scientific application of certain general canons of truth and beauty to particular works of art?" Well, it is a good thing for a dramatic critic to know as much as he can of "the best that has been said and thought" about canons of beauty and truth, and so forth. It is an even better thing, having done so, to be on the alert against regarding himself as a kind of augur, ordained to tell the common man what is what at the theatre, on the strength of this surveying, referring and casting-up business. That way lie pedantry and pretentiousness, unless the augur who inspects the entrails of the particular fowl under review, and compares them with those of an absolute and quintessential fowl laid up in heaven, be a person of most divine modesty and candour.

Every first-rate critic's standard of beauty, if he has such a thing about him, is more or less different from every other's. Standard, indeed, is not the word for it ; it is a tempered sense, a practised capacity for emotion of some sort, in presence of works of art. Mr. Agate has written better than any one else about Bernhardt and also about Marie Lloyd. But the strength of these fine criticisms was not that their writer put any authoritative measuring-tapes to the art of these diverse women of genius. Of course he must have tried for truth of a kind. But it was not truth to any supposed laws or standards of beauty. It was truth to himself as an artist, an expresser of a purely personal sense of fact, the courage of his own impressions, which might, for all that he knew, be those of nobody else.

With all this spirited autonomy, it somehow comes about that good dramatic critics are, as a body, always fighting on one side in a kind of war that never ceases, between good stuff and trash. Every English critic of note strove for the admission of Ibsen to the English stage ; they all trumpeted, in its arduous and stormy dawn, the rising genius of Mr. Shaw ; they were all backers of Mr. Granville Barker at the Court Theatre, of Mr. Yeats and his friends at the Abbey, and of Miss Horniman in Manchester. To-day, they all stand guard on the dykes to prevent a dreary and vulgar lubricity from flooding whole provinces of the stage. So, in a sense, they are banded in an army ; and yet they have not enlisted ; each has only followed the individual artist's golden rule of trusting his own guiding sense of delight. That the result is a large measure of common action shows that, after all, there *is* such a thing as quality in plays and in acting ; through the wide sands of common theatrical rubbish there does flow at least a trickle of fine work, always threatened but never quite broken, and every first-rate critic is found to drink at it with relish.

Also, however little of a conscious propagandist your first-rate critic may be, he does have an effect on the great public which sometimes speaks of him so harshly. Last year, as Mr. Agate recalls, *The Wild Duck* ran for fifty nights ; a popular actress elected to play in *A Doll's House ;* all the four Tchehov plays were acted—and that not on Sundays. So infectious may enjoyment of fine work become, if the enjoyment itself finds fine expression. Sometimes a boy who has never thought of poetry as anything but dead stodge buried in old books will make his first discovery of literature simply by hearing some friend repeat a few lines with a gusto which raises their beauty from the dead. That is the unit of perfect criticism. To make other people like a thing you must delight in it first, and no mere *ex-officio* delight, like a second-rate schoolmaster's delight in Plautus, will do. You must, in the fullest sense of the words, enjoy yourself—first enjoy the actor or the play with all the energies of the delighted spirit, and then, in telling others of this ecstasy, enjoy *yourself*—your brightened wit, the quickened stir of your brain as it seeks the right word or image, the delicious feeling, which all great art arouses in a fit spectator, that you are getting more out of life than was ever promised you at birth or baptism. Art is about oneself ; Mr. Agate is all the better reading to me because he affects no judicial detachment or scientific impersonality. He tinges everything that he describes with the humours of his own mind, and so the thing described comes out better and more likely to stick in the reader's head, as a character does in a novel when he is described by some vivid person in the story, and not by the mere impersonal author. Enjoyment of art, dramatic or other, can only be taught by example, and Mr. Agate is a famous enjoyer.

C. E. MONTAGUE.

# Contents

PAGE

GREEK PLAY

"The Hippolytus of Euripides" . . 3

ELIZABETHAN DRAMA

"Hamlet" . . . . . . 11

"Richard III." . . . . . 17

"Henry VIII." . . . . . 22

"Antony and Cleopatra" . . . 27

"The Tragical History of Doctor Faustus" 31

"The White Devil" . . . . 37

FOREIGN PLAYS AND ADAPTATIONS

"Six Characters in Search of an Author" 45

"Henry IV." . . . . . . 45

"And That's The Truth" . . . 45

"Peer Gynt" . . . . . 60

"A Doll's House" . . . . . 68

"The Wild Duck" . . . . . 73

"The Cherry Orchard" . . . . 77

"The Sea-Gull" . . . . . 83

"The Godless" . . . . . 89

"L'École des Cocottes" . . . . 94

"The Verge" . . . . . 98

# Contents

PAGE

MODERN PLAYS

"Tess of the d'Urbervilles" . . . 105
"The Prisoners of War" . . . . 110
"Juno and the Paycock" . . . . 114
"The Round Table" . . . . 119
"Gloriana" . . . . . . 124
"The Green Hat" . . . . . 129
"Fallen Angels" and "Ariadne, or Business
    First" . . . . . . 134
"Spring Cleaning" . . . . . 140
"The Last of Mrs. Cheyney" . . . 144
"Hay Fever" . . . . . . 149
"Rain" . . . . . . 157
"The Moon and Sixpence" . . . 163
"The Swallow" . . . . . 168
"Overture" . . . . . . 172
"The Torch Bearers" . . . . 177
"Camilla States Her Case" . . . 182
"Lullaby" . . . . . . 186
"Lavender Ladies" . . . . . 190
"Cristilinda" . . . . . . 194
"The Sea Urchin" and "Tarnish" . . 199
"Anyhouse" . . . . . . 204


REVIVALS

"The Rivals" . . . . . 211
"Caste" . . . . . . 215
"On 'Change" . . . . . 220

xii

# Contents

|  |  | PAGE |
|---|---|---|
| " Cæsar and Cleopatra " | . . . . | 224 |
| " Mrs. Warren's Profession " | . . . | 229 |
| " The Madras House " | . . . . | 235 |
| " Iris " | . . . . . . . | 240 |
| " Old Heidelberg " | . . . . . | 245 |
| " Kismet " | . . . . . . | 250 |

## MELODRAMA

| " The Show " | . . . . . . | 259 |
|---|---|---|
| " The Tyrant " | . . . . . | 265 |
| " Ordeal " | . . . . . . | 272 |
| " The River " | . . . . . | 278 |
| " No. 17 " | . . . . . . | 283 |
| " The Ghost Train " | . . . . | 289 |
| " The Shame Woman " | . . . . | 294 |

# Greek Play

# "The Hippolytus of Euripides"

## English Version by GILBERT MURRAY

### Regent Theatre

TIMES change, but not in way of prudery, which is ageless and lays a dull hand alike on Euripides and on Shaw. The first version of *Hippolytus*, in which Phædra acts out of her own volition and is punished, offended the Athenian Watch Committee and had to be withdrawn. In the amended version, Queen, King, and Stepson are pawns in a tiff between two peddling goddesses, Aphrodite and Artemis, which makes the mortals less interesting dramatically and less instructive morally. How Shavianly the old Greek must have laughed in his beard when he set about the job of re-writing! How cunning his revenge, in which he makes out a good case for passion and a wretched one for refraining. *On ne badine pas avec l'amour*, but Euripides shows that it were better to trifle with the goddess than to spurn her altogether. Poor Hippolytus, to have a patroness so feeble, unable to do more than " grieve and stand apart." Meagre consolation for the lad that Trozen's yokeless maids shall

shear their tresses in his memory. A shingler's reward !
Better, Euripides makes us reflect, for the young votary
if he had passed on and paid his attention to the other
goddess. He would have lived to hunt another day.
Which, presumably, is precisely the lesson which the
Athenian greybeards would not have had taught. But
that is Censorship's little way.

Yet it is possible that those old Greeks corrected
more wisely than they knew. It is significant that the
great Clairon, when she played Racine's version from
which the goddesses were deleted, found it necessary
to restore them, at least to the apprehension of the
spectator. " Phèdre's virtue would doubtless overcome
her passion, if that passion were only the normal straying of the senses and the imagination ; it is to the sway
of Venus that Phèdre yields. At the bidding of a
superior power she must do and say that which her
virtue reproves. In every word of the part this
struggle must be made apparent to the spectator's eye
and driven home to his mind." Probably Clairon was
only echoing Racine, who found Phædra neither guilty
nor guiltless, " since her passion is forced upon her both
by destiny and the anger of the gods, *and she is the first
to be moved to horror at it.*" Perhaps Clairon found
the best word for the Queen when she called her a
" somnambule." In the French play Phèdre is largely
in a dream from which she awakens only at death,
thus exciting compassion as for a child punished for
something it has not done. Bernhardt followed
Clairon closely here, representing Phèdre as a pure

soul who, if she had not been lashed by the goddess, wanted only to be " good." Rachel, on the other hand, is believed to have laid most stress on the scenes of self-loathing and denunciation, and Miss Thorndike's reading inclines to that of Rachel. Her Queen has not Bernhardt's fever of passion wearing the soul away, with intervals for ineffable wistfulness and pathos. It has not the child-like quality. It is even a trifle *bourgeoise*, and you feel that the poor creature is thoroughly sensible at heart, and may at any moment come to her senses and give Hippolytus a talking to for his priggishness.

To tell the truth, in the Greek Phædra is not a particularly good part. When the curtain goes up on Euripides' play the drama, as far as Phædra is concerned is virtually over. In the wretched woman's mind everything has already happened that can happen. She is absolute for death—" My poor limbs scarce obey me now "—and only dying remains. But when the French Phèdre says :

> N'allons point plus avant ; demeurons, chère Œnone !
> Je ne me soutiens plus, ma force m'abandonne . . .

we, knowing our great French actresses, must decline to believe her. We know that Phèdre's strength will not give out till her impersonator has squeezed the last drop of effect from the first-act indictment of Venus, the second act declaration to Hippolyte, the long-drawn scene of jealousy of his sweetheart and the sighing after sunrise " clear and serene," and that late, last fifth act of expiatory syncope. The idea of suicide does not

strike Phèdre till close upon midnight.    Now
Euripides, who foresaw not Clairon, is entitled to reply
that his play is not really about Phædra at all, but about
Hippolytus, and that the *scène-à-faire* is between father
and son.    There is no answer to this, and it explains
why Miss Thorndike cannot make much out of the part.
Moral indignation and elder pathos are this actress's
*forte*—see her Hecuba—and in this play these are
implied rather than formulated.    The supernatural
bondage is suggested not at all, but Miss Thorndike may
very well argue that the goddesses are there in person,
and that even in Greek tragedy it is no use keeping a
dog and barking oneself.

But the acting in these old plays must, like the pro-
verbial pudding, contain at least one succulent and
splendacious plum.    Mr. Nicholas Hannen's Hippolytus supplied the needful here.    He presented a superb
picture of the paragon—Galahad, Lohengrin, Bayard,
and whichever of Sandford and Merton was the good
little boy, all rolled into one.    His hero had all the
insolent intolerance of the very young ; you felt that
his virtue was as the virtue of ten, because his heart was
so very pure and his head so very thick.    A good coach-
ing by Dumas *fils* in the school of *tout comprendre, c'est
tout pardonner* might perhaps have taught him how to
turn that particular corner without a spill, physical or
moral.    (Admitted that there would then have been
no play.)    Mr. Hannen presented his youthful
phenomenon in the fashion permitted only to great
artists, dazzling the eye as with a nimbus, and painting

6

the soul by a plentiful disobedience of Browning's
injunction not to mind the arms and legs. His every
pose might have served a Praxiteles, and his dying had
the austerity of marble. Mr. Casson can play any
Greek Messenger standing on his head, but I do not
feel that Theseus need be quite such a bore as Mr.
Leahy suggested.

Mr. Bruce Winston's costumes delighted the eye, as
always ; and, personally, I care nothing for mere
accuracy in this matter. The whole production was
excellent, though from where I sat the statue of
Aphrodite looked like a composite figure of Miss Nellie
Wallace's lodging-house keeper and Miss Murdstone
confronting Betsey Trotwood. Artemis, on the other
side of the Palace, was not unlike the latter.

*February* 24.

# Elizabethan Drama

# " Hamlet "

## By WILLIAM SHAKESPEARE

### Haymarket Theatre

MOODS may be of many kinds, and Hamlet undoubtedly had his fair-weather ones. *Au fond*, this young man was of an amiable, lively, and even sunny disposition. How, else, could Ophelia have drawn up that shining catalogue? Or how, if his Prince's heart had been otherwise, could the frank and manly Horatio have won to it? But Shakespeare, who never hit the nail except on the head, has already settled this beyond any argument in that one-line epitaph. " Noble " and " sweet " are Horatio's adjectives, nothing being said about melancholy. Is not the case a plain one of transfusion, the dejection being Shakespeare's? Put it the other way round. Is there a single line of the Sonnets which might not have been penned by Hamlet in one or other of his moods?

This is only to reiterate the old statement that Hamlet is Shakespeare himself—a commonplace, doubtless, but one to be borne in mind whenever an actor reissues the old, magnificent challenge. It is the familiar affair of dual superlatives—the glorious morning obscured by basest clouds, " heavenly alchemy," and " ugly wrack." Can the actor essaying Hamlet give us both aspects—the sky of bluest blue and the sweeping storms of darkest pessimism ? Can he compass the tenderness of the " heart's core " peech, the filial piety, the polished courtesy and badinage, the sinister preoccupation, the nosing after corruption, the ranting and mouthing ? Can he, in a word, pour into this great part all the treasures of the richest of human minds ? Has he the physical perfections, the romantic riches, to pour ? But Hamlet's mind has ugliness also, and your actor must in his person exhibit these as well. Mr. Barrymore's Hamlet draws fewer tears than Robertson's, but it is nearer to Shakespeare's whole creation than any other I have seen. In fact, this *is* Hamlet, since you have but to scratch the god and the demon instantly appears.

What are Mr. Barrymore's qualifications ? Well, first a handsome face, intellectual as to the brow, a trifle womanish in the lower part, after the manner of the paintings of Angelica Kauffmann. Next an agreeable voice, touching nobility here and there, but lacking the organ-note and in emotion running too easily to the head-notes of the tenor. Add the purest diction, perfect enunciation, and unexampled clarity. Now note a slim figure and the general illusion of princeliness and youth. All these are informed—and here is the key—by intellectual capacity of a rare order and analytical power of extreme cogency.

How, with such gifts, does Shakespeare's poetry

fare ? A trifle ill is the answer. Mr. Barrymore has the finest possible sense of values in the case of single words. Take such a line as " How weary, stale, flat, and unprofitable . . . " and note how it is built up of successive images which come into the mind before the word is coined to represent them. The actor never gabbles. But this good quality may have its corresponding defect, by which I do not mean want of pace alone, but of power to sweep the listener off his feet. Mr. Barrymore builds lines out of words, but he does not always weld the lines into the whole which a great speech must be. The first and third soliloquies are ratiocinative, the second—" O, what a rogue and peasant slave am I ! "—belongs surely to the domain of pure emotion. It is a cadenza, a piece of virtuosity, an exercise in what musicians call *rubato*.

This is the speech in which Hamlet is to prepare the spectator for his " Get-thee-to-a-nunnery " tirades, and Ophelia's " blasted with ecstasy." Mr. Barrymore blasted it with pure reason. You felt that he saw himself first as a rogue, than as a slave, who, moreover, must take on the attributes of a *peasant* slave. He made note one by one of all the aspects of a player who should simulate grief—the tears, distraction, and broken voice. But Hamlet is at white heat, or working up to it, and the debating method does not carry us away. It is possible that this achievement is not within this actor's scope, but I submit that a declamatory failure would here be better than expository success. The sails of the actor's voice having no knack of bellying, Mr.

Barrymore attempts to get power by sudden gusts, choosing a single word for an explosion. Sometimes the choice is quite arbitrary, as in his refusal to take the King when he is " fit and seasoned for his passage." Passage is the word chosen here, and the violence is without meaning. Certain it is that Mr. Barrymore cannot cope with such words as " this majestical roof fretted with golden fire." His Hamlet has too much the *indoor* look, as the essayist remarked of Raphael's figures, and will find his images in his own brain. Such a one would not rack the heavens for a comparison. Sun and stars are not his concern, and the words, being perfunctory, are robbed of their just splendour.

But I have given too much space to fault-finding. The play-scene was immensely fine, its climax being a miracle of virtuosity, and the closet-scene was perfection. Much of the latter was spoken on Gertrude's breast, and the pathos was overpowering. And from here right on to the end I thought the performance magnificent. It gathered power, coherence, and cumulative effect ; in short, we knew ourselves to be in the presence of a fine and powerful mind. But surely the savagery and tang of the end is lost unless the quarrel with Laertes takes place where Shakespeare explicitly directs that it shall take place. At the words " This is I, Hamlet, the Dane ! " Hamlet *must* leap into the grave. This is a giant's conception, and the vaunt in " the Dane " is to prepare us for the vault. The actor made amends with a duel in which he was half impish and half " fey." At the realisation

of Laertes's treachery we saw him gather up decision ;
he spitted the King with gusto, and in his own dying
found felicity. The whole performance had a hundred
little perceptivities and touches, and no perversities of
ingenuity. Only once was Mr. Barrymore naughty,
when, at the words " crawling between heaven and
earth," he indicated that the former was situated in
Ophelia's hair. To sum up, this was a great though
not an overwhelming performance. The magnanimity
of genius was not present, and at times mere conscientiousness threatened her pale wing. But all that intellect could do was done.

The cast was brilliant almost throughout. Perfec-
tion is not too complete a word for Miss Constance
Collier's Queen, admirably " lived," yet low in key.
Would Mr. Augustus John paint another " Tragic
Muse " ? Here is his subject and his colour. Miss
Fay Compton's Ophelia was fragrant, wistful, and had
a child's importunacy, unmatched in my time. Mr.
Courtenay Thorpe's anguishing Ghost was authenti-
cally from another world, and spoke a music rare in
this. Mr. Malcolm Keen made a good King, Mr.
Waring a fair Polonius, Mr. Ben Field a creditable
grave-digger, and Mr. Shayle Gardner a cherubic
Fortinbras. A word is due to the Osric of Mr.
Frederick Cooper and the Bernardo of Mr. Roy
Travers, a tiny part excellently played.

But few lines are left for the setting of the American
Mr. Robert Edmund Jones. I declare this to be the
most beautiful thing I have ever seen on any stage

The vast arch at the back served as the battlements, and was hung with curtains for the indoor scenes, played on two platforms intersecting a flight of steps. Up these Ophelia had to make a final exit of great peril, achieved by Miss Compton with immense skill and nerve. But should not the churchyard scene of Mr. Norman Wilkinson have the melancholy of summer afternoons ? The dark and the cold may be more accurate, but the mind is thereby frozen with horror, when it should melt with pity.

*February* 19.

# " Richard III "

## By WILLIAM SHAKESPEARE

### The " Old Vic "

"RICHARD III." is really a boy's play—a play for one boy to write and another to see. It belongs to the poet's first period, and we behold in it the germ of things to be amplified later on. Thus Richard's

> But I am in
> So far in blood that sin will pluck on sin.

is to become Macbeth's

> I am in blood
> Stepp'd in so far that, should I wade no more,
> Returning were as tedious as go o'er.

Sin plucking on sin is a philosophical common-place, whereas real heart-ache is in " tedious." Compare

> There is no creature loves me ;
> And if I die, no soul will pity me.

with the greater pathos of all that passage about the sear, the yellow leaf. This early play is full of indications of the greatness to come. Is there not something of complicated Angelo in Richard's two wooings ? There is a kind of ghoulish gusto about the scene with

Anne which half suggests that the poet held at one time
the more sadistic view of Richard as a man delighting in
villainy for its own sake.   But the idea seems to have
been quickly dropped, and after this one scene Richard
comes back to the simple *rôle* of opportunist-murderer,
sorting one " pitchy day " after another for such as
stand in his light.   Richard wanted the sun, the whole
sun, and nothing but the sun, and that is why the tale
becomes so simple.   You feel as you watch the play
that Marryat or Ballantyne, or any other dependable
writer for boys, could have put the bones of it together.
But it would be wrong to mistake the Crookback for
an early Captain Hook.   There is a kind of actor who
sees in Richard, not a Gilles de Rais but an ogre out of
the story-books murdering little children in their beds
for the innocent fun of the thing.   Such a Richard,
says Lamb, is very close and shrewd, and devilish
cunning, for you can see that by his eye.   But there is
more in the character than this.   There is the poet, be-
trayed by the romantic splendour of thought expressing
itself in such phrases as those about the aspiring blood
of Lancaster, and the aery building in the cedar's top.
Everything about Richard is magnificent.   His mental
quality matches his physical courage, so that he may be
said not to act, but to magnoperate.   We demand for
him at the end, not the gallows, but the Judgment Seat.

How much of all this does Mr. Baliol Holloway
give ?   Well, first his Richard is a man, and not a
mental abstraction.   Next, he is a man of genius set
apart from his fellows by superiority of mind and will.

Then, again, he is alive, and alive in his own century and not in ours.   But I do not, alas ! find the poet in this Richard, owing probably to the actor's indifferent mastery of verse.   Mr. Holloway still persists in cutting up every speech into granulated nodules, though this habit is less persistent than it was.   Yet it maintains sufficiently to stand in the way of that full swoop and rush of delighted words which mark the poet.   If one must continue for a little in the matter of shortcomings, one would say that Mr. Holloway failed to excite either pity or terror.   He did not melt us in the tent scene, but then we are to remember that many Richards, including Edwin Booth, have failed here.   Nor did the actor quite succeed in making the " seated heart knock at the ribs."   He lacked the cold malignancy of Irving, and also something of the stunning power of sheer noise.   When Booth played the scene with Hastings we are told that he turned furiously on the latter's " if " and hammered the courtier's death-knell upon the table with blows of the sceptre which struck terror into every heart.   In short, our friend's performance wanted a touch of the fiend.

But there is a great deal in it that is immensely good. Mr. Holloway makes that incredible wooing credible ; he listens to Margaret's curses in a silence of admirable mockery ; he toys with Buckingham like a very large cat with a particularly small mouse, and plays the " I am not in the giving vein to-day " scene as well as it need be played.   Throughout one is conscious of Richard's master mind, buoyant spirit, and all that knowledge of man and character which the part contains. Mr. Holloway's closing scenes, like Kean's, are the most brilliant. Like the older actor, he has given to all the busy scenes of the play the greatest animation and effect. He has filled every part of the stage, and pleased the eye with a succession of splendid robes and striking attitudes. His costumes have been blood-red, and red blood has run in this capital tyrant. Now comes the fight, which is done with immense vigour. Kean is said to have stood after his sword was taken from him with his hands stretched out in a pose of preternatural and terrific grandeur, as if his will-power alone was more than a match for Richmond's steel. Mr. Holloway has a marvellous facial expression when he turns and sees his sixth and last Richmond. At that moment all the venom of the bottled spider rushes to his face, which takes on a superhuman ugliness. His Wednesday night onslaught and overthrow was a great piece of work, almost lifting one out of one's seat. As the actor lay panting on the ground one played with the thought that there was in that body still sufficient of the dregs of life to taste the bitterness of defeat. If the rest of the part had been acted up to this level one would have saluted a performance of genius. But though genius is not the word one would use, Mr. Holloway's acting was undoubtedly fine.

Miss Edith Evans gave Queen Margaret's two scenes with a great sweep of passion and magnificence of diction. Here is an actress who can walk like a queen and rant like one also. We owe the " Old Vic " a debt for teaching Miss Thorndike to be a great actress ; in descending upon this theatre in the full plenitude of her powers Miss Evans repays that debt.    But the team at the " Old Vic " had rather too much tail.    Mr. Duncan Yarow made a conscientious Clarence, though one associates the playing of this part with something more liquid in grace and beauty.    It is perhaps not disparaging to say that Mr. Neil Porter endowed Buckingham with a nose of more than Roman loftiness, and he certainly spoke his lines as though he intended the back of the pit to hear them.    The two murderers were played uncommonly well by Messrs. Charles Marford and John Garside.    Some of the other young gentlemen in the cast were amateurish, which fault time, perhaps, will remove.

The piece was done in admirably devised settings. Perhaps Richard's tent was not very well suggested, the ghostly victims wearing something of the air of a collection from Madame Tussaud's.    Either Mr. Holloway omitted the words " the lights burn blue," or I did not hear them.    One remembers how Mr. Atkins said them, and how the mind was suddenly filled with the colour of the night sky.    There was a touch of imagination here which the play's present production does not quite give.

*October 7.*

# " Henry VIII "

## By WILLIAM SHAKESPEARE

### Empire Theatre

WHOEVER wrote this play managed to get an
extraordinary number of fine things into it,
though unity of impression is not one of them.    Why
should it be ?    The play is not called the " bloodie
tragedie " of somebody or other, but declares itself
simply as " The Famous History of the Life of King
Henry the Eight."    There are lots of things in this
chronicle which can never be tidied up into any formal
play—the passing of the Middle Ages and last kick of
Rome, the rise of Protestantism and the growth of this
country from a third to a first-rate power.    One does
not mean that the characters babble, or are even conscious of, these swelling themes.    They do not, like the
soldier in the melodrama, strike their breasts and
declare that they are off to the Thirty Years War.

It will be argued that it is through our own minds,
and not through the actual words of this play, that the
Middle Ages blow ; " there is not a breath of mediæval
atmosphere in Shakespeare's histories " has trumpeted
Mr. Shaw.    And he goes on to tell us that Shakespeare's

kings are not statesmen, that his cardinals have no religion, and that his plays contain no hint that the world is finally governed by forces expressing themselves in laws rather than by vulgar individuals expressing themselves in rows. This is as it may be ; and possibly we who, seeing this play, put into it something that is not there, are entitled to reflect how fortunate it is that Shakespeare, who would never have pretended to half Mr. Shaw's understanding of history, had some skill as a depicter of vulgar rows to fall back upon.

Can there be any doubt that Katharine's three scenes are as moving as anything in Shakespeare ? Maiden virtue rudely strumpeted has always been a sure card with the tear-compellers, but is there not even greater poignancy when the virtue is wifely ? The most pitiful pages in that great novel *La Cousine Bette* are those which concern the woes of the pious Adeline. Yet we find Hulot writing to his enchantress, Madame Marneffe : " My wife has never, throughout twenty-five years, interfered with my pleasures. Yet to you I would sacrifice a hundred Adelines ! " There, surely, speaks the very voice of Henry ! How comes it, then, that this infamous gormandiser is not the villain of the piece ? Is it not that we regard him as something which is as little moral or immoral as a volcano ? " Chastity," says Stevenson of the elder Dumas, " was not dear to the heart of this ventripotent mulatto." Nor to Henry, from whose loins were to spring Elizabeth and England's greatest age. We look upon him solely in his quality of begetter, and feel that to try his potency at the bar of private virtue is to bring the matter to the wrong court. But the drama needs a villain whose discomfiture shall compensate us for the Queen's martyrdom, and Wolsey fills the breach. How any play can be considered long or boring which contains this trio—one of whom is a magnificent essay in *goguenarderie*—passes my comprehension. Add the moving incident of Buckingham and the bugles of greatness-to-come blowing faintly but surely, and it seems to me that dullness can only be in the mind of the beholder. It lacks poetry ? One would retort that a horse need not be good-looking to win a race.

How was the piece played ? Queen Katharine is not generally considered a great part, but Miss Thorndike showed that greatness may be brought to it. This artist proved once more that there is only one answer to the question as to whether she is a great actress. The answer is : " Yes, in a great play." Her features may not launch ships for light-hearted capture ; let them show moral anguish and whole navies will flock to her succour. Her voice is not for balconies and conquests, yet in suffering moves you to shattering depths of spiritual pity. In sporting parlance this actress cannot " come without the horse," and in second-rate plays her talents are not of the first order. But let a great dramatist cry " Ho ! " and this fine artist will give him successful battle. Her manner then changes, infelicity drops from her, and she puts on the whole armour of artistry. Anything more noble, more dignified, more womanly, or more truly heroical than this Katherine it would be impossible to conceive ; and in the ringing challenge of the trial scene Miss Thorndike may be said to have touched the sublime.

The first five minutes of Mr. Norman V. Norman's Henry were a little disappointing. There was the mischievous thought that this was going to be a study of the bluff king as Mr. Stanley Lupino might impishly present him ; there was even the hint of barn-door crowing in this old rooster's turn of the head and cock of the eye. But the uncertain moment soon passed, and from Henry's second appearance everything went magnificently. Here were the authentic traits— sensuality, cruelty, arrogance, humour. And the fellow had temperament to boot. The playing of two of the other big parts finds me in some difficulty. One respected the Wolsey of Mr. E. Lyall Swete, whose fine performance as Warwick obviously paved the way for the Cardinal. But was this quite the Wolsey who ruled England ? This figure lacked something of grandeur and awe ; he suggested the prelate hardly at all ; and one would always have backed Mrs. Proudie to rout him. The trouble was one largely of voice, too richly comic and at times recalling Mr. Bransby Williams. Mr. Arthur Wontner's Buckingham seemed to me at once " actorish " and ineffectual ; one was too busy noting the airs and graces to feel any tug at the heartstrings. Let it be said that this absence of reaction was purely personal, and was not general in the house, which gave both performers a magnificent ovation.

## The Contemporary Theatre

I am afraid I thought the Anne Bullen of that clever artist, Miss Angela Baddeley, too childish and too slight. She looked about fifteen, while Anne's age at her coronation is given at the earliest as twenty-six, and is placed by some authorities at thirty-one. And the actress's physique could only give the lie to the Third Gentleman's description. All the smaller parts were well filled, Miss Ada King in particular contributing a little cameo which, as one thinks of it, defies any kind of appraisement. There is no question here of better or best ; the ribald dame simply walked out of the sixteenth century as out of a frame. Mr. Bruce Winston, as a *vieux cancanier*, was finely of the period.

The whole production was put on with all the care, enthusiasm, and insight which spell Casson. The setting by Mr. Charles Ricketts came in for general commendation, though, personally, I cannot shout my loudest here. I find something in this artist's view of the times which will not let me believe that the oak was growing which was to defeat the Armada. Stained glass windows and a colour-scheme inclining to claret are admittedly pleasant, and I expect to be told that the date is pre-Elizabeth, and that this French atmosphere is correct. But I have the feeling that it is the early sixteenth century seen through the eyes of the late nineteenth.

*December* 23.

26

# "Antony and Cleopatra"

## By WILLIAM SHAKESPEARE

### THE "OLD VIC"

SO little was cut out of this piece that one almost fears the management of the "Old Vic" has succumbed to the fetish of performing these plays as they were written. One or two small scenes might certainly have gone, and so long an interval between the dying of the two protagonists is certain to make for anticlimax. One feels that just as the same grave was made to clip the pair, so their deaths should be close in time. Perhaps this is to have too much respect for Cleopatra : and there may be irony in the scene in which she has that vulgar row with her treasurer in the presence of Cæsar. But the end of a tragedy is no place for irony which delays the action, and a capital motto for all Shakespearean producers is Cleopatra's own, " resolution and the briefest end."

The best Cleopatra I ever saw was Janet Achurch, who was equally overpowering whether she did a thing immensely right or immensely wrong. Mr. Shaw put it on record that everything that Janet did as Cleopatra was mistaken, but the fact remains that her performance was unforgettable. There was majesty and there was physical passion ; there were looks which might have unpeopled a city, and tones which might have quelled provinces. Miss Edith Evans administers none of these shocks. "Which is the Queen of Egypt ? " asks Cæsar, on entering the Monument, and, indeed, the jade is never very easily distinguished from her attendants. Miss Evans appears to have purposely stressed the childish element in Cleopatra ; at times even she seemed to be imitating Miss Ffrangçon Davies's spoilt child of the other play. Miss Evans's genius for lofty scorn for once found itself misplaced ; this actress, who can do wonders among the magnani-mities, was baffled by a part in which the magnanimous is not even glimpsed. I take it that any actress who is to play Cleopatra should show us the most primitive of emotions worked up to its last subtlety of acquired finesse. "Her genius," wrote a great critic of Réjane, "was sex bejewelled with every invention of cunning and charm that in civilised history—perhaps long before—the instinct has forged for its armoury ; so that you felt she was the last, up-to-date, of the line of Helen and Sappho and Queen Cleopatra and Mary Stewart, and all the women famous in history for womanishness. The craft which spoke in her voice and her eyes was the sum and perfection of what, in all but the most noble ages, most men have wished woman to have instead of high intellect." But that is very exactly not Miss Evans's *forte*. She has not enough passion and vulgarity for Cleopatra, or you may say that she has too much fastidiousness. This was a Queen of Egypt who had read Paul Bourget. Brilliant comédienne though Miss Evans is, she has not a great deal of pathos, and it was Antony in his scene with Eros and not Cleopatra in her last scene with her dying lover, who drew the tears of the house. I need not say that what brains and skill could do was achieved. But the actress was simply not suited.

Mr. Baliol Holloway played Antony as well, one thinks, as that difficult part could be played. He looked very noble and debonair, and perhaps—though I am not quite sure—beneath his charm of manner he was sufficiently vacillating and dissolute. The actor gave the poetry of his lines well, and was very moving in places, though he did not get the full pathos out of " Bring to me all my sad captains," and had not sufficient power, pace, and excitement for the passage about the Hill of Basan. Antony here out-roared the horned herd too much like a bull who is not sure of his next line. But the performance was very good on the whole, as is everything which this clever actor attempts. Mr. Neil Porter made a very effective Enobarbus, and succeeded in delivering the most threadbare tag in Shakespeare as though it were newly minted in his mind. Mr. Duncan Yarrow gave Cæsar dignity ; and it is well that he did for this character possesses no other sort of interest. Pompey struck me as being capable, when in mufti, of the indiscretion known as Oxford bags. All the other young men did fairly well, and indeed to give identity to these Shakespearean odds and ends is a difficult task.

I am afraid I thought that the piece was rather meagrely put on. If ever a Shakespearean play calls for music, processions, and Tadema-like excesses in bathroom marble, *Antony and Cleopatra* is that play. Whereas, so far as I could see, Alexandria and Rome only possessed two pieces of furniture between them, and the population of these cities was about three to the square mile. Owing to the peculiarly cold quality of the lighting the Egyptian temperature seemed to be a good ten degrees below freezing point. Also, I did definitely object to Cleopatra's refusal to die sitting bolt upright on a throne. This is obviously the proper thing to do. Any objection that the Monument did not contain a throne would be frivolous ; neither, probably, did it contain Cleopatra's robe and crown. And I submit that she would certainly not have bothered to put these on if she was going to curl up and die on the sofa like a naughty consumptive in the reign of Dumas *fils*.

*November* 30.

# " The Tragical History of Doctor Faustus "

## By CHRISTOPHER MARLOWE

### THE PHŒNIX SOCIETY

THERE are other reasons besides the likeness to
Mr. Walkley—" And live and die in Aristotle's
works "—which incline us to regard Faustus as a Great
Man. His tragedy is that of all the Shakespearean
protagonists—the overthrow of a soul essentially noble.
The lust of Faustus is the lust for something of vaster
scope than material pleasure. He would rule a world
of honour and omnipotence, command all things that
move between the quiet poles, enjoy dominion stretch-
ing as far as the mind of man. It will certainly occur
to those whose conception of this great legend has been
vitiated by Gounod's operatic trash, and it may occur
to others as well, that Faustus did not get very much
out of his bargain with the Devil, which was to live " in
all voluptuousness " for four-and-twenty years. Faustus
plans to bridge the moving air, which is an engineer's
project, and to make Spain and Africa contributory to

his crown, which is the dream of a Napoleon or a Rhodes. But in the subsequent play these things are not realised ; while to indulge in a Pageant of Sinfulness and play tricks on the Pope and a horse-coper seem to be less part of a philosophic scheme than a desire to entertain the groundlings. One feels that even a confirmed money-grubber would be able to find pleasure more exciting than a personally-conducted tour through Italy. The play, in short, waits for Helen and for all that Helen means to your *homme moyen sensuel*.

But now the great poet in Marlowe takes hold of the playwright and turns the bodily presence of the world's paramour into air and cloud. It is interesting to compare the description of Helen given in the prose *History*. The author of this translation from the German *Volksbuch* tells us that she wore a most rich gown of purple velvet, costly embroidered. Her hair, fair as beaten gold, was " of such length that it reached down to her hams " ; her eyes were " amorous and cole-black." The account of this beauty is as matter of fact as Gautier's catalogue of the Ideal Mistress who shall not discard ring or bracelet, and whose dress may not be less than brocade. Our prose historian goes on to say that his heroine " looked about her with a rolling hawke's eye and smiling wanton countenance, which near-hand inflamed the hearts of all the students, but that they persuaded themselves she was a spirit, which made them lightly pass away such fancies." So Marlowe purifies his spectator's spirit by dissolving

32

Helen into pure poetry.   One would make bold and
say  that

> Sweet Helen, make me immortal with a kiss,
> Her lips suck forth my soul ; see where it flies !—
> Come, Helen, come, give me my soul again.
> Here will I dwell, for Heaven is in these lips,
> And all is dross that is not Helena,

has a glory of pure passion not exceeded even in *Antony
and Cleopatra*, and that the ethereal quality of

> Oh, thou art fairer than the evening air
> Clad in the beauty of a thousand stars ;
> Brighter art thou than flaming Jupiter
> When he appeared to hapless Semele :
> More lovely than the monarch of the sky
> In wanton Arethusa's azured arms :

is not excelled even by the Flower Speech of Perdita.
And if one must be quoting and comparing one would
suggest that the last speech of Faustus, containing the
famous

> See, see where Christ's blood streams in the firmament !
> One drop would save my soul—half a drop : ah, my Christ !

is not to be beaten anywhere in Shakespeare.   I have
always had the fancy—though this is probably highly
uncritical—that the image of the streaming firmament
was suggested by the sunset shining in the player's face.
We know that the piece was originally performed in a
playhouse half-open to the sky, and that the performances took place in the late afternoon.   I do not stress
the point, for the objection is obvious that the hour is

between eleven and midnight. But that mattered little at a time when night and darkness had to be suggested in full sunshine by the presence on the stage of a flaming torch. Yet obviously the line has the suggestion of the last sunset upon which the doomed man is to gaze.

The Phœnix Society did the play very well, probably as effectively as it ever can be done with a purely formalised stage. Is it all, until we draw near to the two great passages at the end, a trifle bare in interest ? We have ceased to believe in the devils which were real to the Elizabethan audience, and in the magic which still held something of truth for Marlowe. Leave the Ghost out of *Hamlet* and you impair the play very little, whereas the whole of *Faustus* is bound up with the belief in the actual existence of hideous things with tails. An Elizabethan audience had terror painted on half its face and amusement on the other half, whereas we to-day are neither amused nor affrighted. Perhaps we may be justified in thinking th t if Marlowe had known of the resources of the modern theatre he would have turned his Procession of the Seven Deadly Sins into a ballet after the manner of Flecker or Sir Herbert Tree. But severity is the Phœnix note, and in that idiom the performance could not, one thinks, have been materially improved. The Faustus of Mr. Ion Swinley showed once more how wrong it is for this fine romantic actor to make petty descent from Olympus. Mr. Swinley has almost everything that a great player should have—poise, gesture, manner, looks, voice, and diction.

He lacks two things only, pathos and a perfect recollection of his lines. But even so the actor shows intellectual mastery and the power of scaling heights with his author. Mr. Swinley does not entirely succeed in shaking our souls in the great speech at the end ; but he obviously shakes his own, which in these days is no small matter. What a part for Irving was Faustus !

The Mephistopheles of Mr. Ernest Thesiger was flawless. Here, too, the conception is of a spirit fallen from nobleness, and of a hell whose fiends are filled not with delight but with weariness. This actor gave every line of his part its uttermost meaning, so that the words " for where we are is Hell " had the directness of a shaft sunk into the infernal regions. Mr. Thesiger must forgive me if my mind again harks back to Irving. What a wonderful Lesurques-Dubose affair the old man would have made of this play, and how astonishing that he did not have it tinkered up to that end ! We are always told that the comic passages in this piece are interpolations by another hand, but Mr. Hay Petrie made us think otherwise. This actor is either a genius or he is nothing, and his Robin comes easily into the former category. The enormous cast was thickly dotted with good names, and one would not willingly conclude without mention of the admirable performances of Messrs. Bruce Winston, Alexander Field, John Gielgud, Charles Bond, H. R. Hignett, and of Mesdames Leah Bateman, Beatrice Wilson, Florence Saunders and Elsa Lanchester. The stage pictures and grouping throughout were very fine, and from the moment when the curtain revealed Mr. Swinley seated at his books on a dais like some Dante troubled of flesh and spirit the eye was mightily delighted.

*October 25.*

# " The White Devil "

## By JOHN WEBSTER

### Renaissance Theatre

Polonius : " Will you walk out of the air, my lord ? "
Hamlet : " Into my grave ? "

MR. GERALD GOULD, following Plato, to whose apron-strings it would appear that we are to be tied for ever, has been telling us that a great picture " is one which reveals essential goodness, rectifies for mortal hearts the extravagant error and evil of the world, and restores to the pulse and spirit a sense of infinite and absolute harmony." This is a fine sentence, and I wish I could believe it. For if, as Plato maintains, the source of all beauty and greatness is one, then this definition should apply equally to all the arts. And here I rebel. I am inclined to doubt the validity of a definition which covers too many things, definition thereby losing itself in a cloud of well-meaning. For the life of me I cannot see any link between great painting and revelation of essential goodness, or between a great symphony and rebuke of the world's evil. I should be more inclined to call a picture great whose qualities of balance and rhythm

reminded one of the orderly progress of the stars, and a
piece of music great which tempted one to believe that
in their motion the orbs like angels sing.    Surely there
is too much of priggishness in Mr. Gould's dictum
to fit it to the purely emotional arts?    What is
the essential goodness revealed by Titian's *Bacchus and
Ariadne*?    Where is the rebuke to evil in Wagner's
*Tristan and Isolda*?    Drama, with its direct relation
to conduct, is different.    There one would accept such
a definition.

To descend from Shakespeare to Webster is to walk
out of air into the grave, to leave the workaday world of
good and evil for the charnel house of perfect corruption.    In the blackest of Shakespeare's tragedies you
still feel that there is a heaven, and that God is in it.
But in such a play as *The White Devil* there is no heaven
for God to be in ;  evil by becoming normal has ceased
to be extravagant, and goodness no longer is.    It is
difficult to see in Vittoria Corombona anything beyond
the " vamp " of the American film.    It is true that she
is married to a popinjay and is in love with the handsome
Brachiano ;  but there is no kind of conflict n her soul,
and she prepares the murder of her husband and her
lover's lawful wife with the same cold-blooded gusto
with which she would afterwards despatch her brother
Flamineo.    As we watch this play we cannot help
thinking how differently Shakespeare would have
treated the unhappy passion of Vittoria and her duke.
He, we feel, would have made another *Macbeth* of this
theme, and by working out tragedy to its remorseful

end have revealed the essential goodness ordaining that such things shall not be.

But Webster's lovers do not work out their own damnation, and at no time in the play are they conscious of it. Their end comes upon them neither out of themselves nor from their sin ; it is pure mischance. Or, if not mischance, one would say that punishment depends from a scheme of vengeance too loosely knit to be tragic. A strange, decayed Count, one Lodovico, wanders through the play. He has been banished by the Duke of Florence, and his grudge against Vittoria is that she did not induce Brachiano to plead for his pardon. What he has against Brachiano is not clear, but it is this neglected, desultory gentleman who is chosen by Webster to slay the lovers with the help of Brachiano's wife's brother, who for no discoverable reason disguises himself as a Moor. The plot, you see, is complicated, and it is difficult for the spectator to be muddled and moved at the same time.

The Renaissance Theatre had clarified the text a good deal, and possibly a little too much. In the original the murders of Isabella and Camillo are revealed in dumb show to Brachiano by a conjuror, Isabella being made to kiss her husband's portrait which has been previously poisoned, and Camillo having his neck broken during a vaulting match. This dumb show is exactly in the vein of the dead hand, the Masque of Madmen, and Bosola's coffin, cords, and bell in *The Duchess of Malfi*. One suggests that the attempt to bring Webster by omission into touch with sweet and

Shakespearean reason was to diminish him. Probably the best way to enjoy this gloomy dramatist is to put the greater man out of mind and concentrate on the things that are Webster's and Webster's alone. First, then, one would cite his mastery of the apparatus of horror, the vigour of his personages and his prose, and that tumult of being which reminds one of life lived in a moral stoke-hold or black engine-room. Or you might look upon this writer as a kind of tall Agrippa dipping his Shock-headed Peters in the ink-pot. In this play only one or two escape. There is Marcello, brother to Flamineo, and there are also the old woman Cornelia and the child Giovanni. These are, indeed, flowers of the purest and most human pathos. Certainly Giovanni's

> " What do the dead do, uncle ? do they eat,
>    Hear music, go a hunting, and be merry,
>    As we that live ? "

has nothing to fear by comparison with any child-passage in Shakespeare. Webster, master of a prose which ripples like the muscles in a statue of Rodin and of a verse solidifying as we read into marble and bronze, is seldom the poet of gentleness and melancholy. Yet the dirge beginning—

> Call for the robin redbreast and the wren,

is a poem of absolute beauty. Lamb compares it to that other dirge in the *Tempest*—" as that is of the water, watery ; so this is of the earth, earthy." The comparison is just ; both poems do indeed seem to resolve themselves into the elements of which they treat. Webster must have been conscious of having achieved a fine thing here. For he at once empties his stage and gives to Flamineo, whose mind up to this point has been as black as that of Shakespeare's Aaron, these significant lines :—

> I have a strange thing in me, to the which
> I cannot give a name, without it be
> Compassion.

These few human moments apart, one feels that in this play Webster's relation to essential goodness never gets beyond the line—

> The last good deed he did, he pardoned murder.

Mr. Esmé Percy played Brachiano with all that show of beauty and display of temperament which the portrayal of a Florentine noble of the period demands. He made of his penultimate death scene—for Webster is generous in this matter—a smiling, ineffable affair which showed how much of his art this actor learned from Sarah Bernhardt. Miss Laura Cowie's Vittoria was all her own, in so far as it was not a portrait by Holbein, and in this part she showed the best of her intellectual mastery and perfect technique. Mr. Cedric Hardwicke gave a careful study of Flamineo. Mr. Terence O'Brien made a dignified figure of the Cardinal, and Mr. Charles Carson did very well as the bereaved Francisco until in the fourth act his disguise compelled him to minstrelsy of the Moore and Burgess order. Miss Viola Tree made a very weeping-willow of Isabella, and in a long cast one would feel inclined to mention specially Mesdames Marie Ault, Rose Quong, and Patricia Hayes. Mr. George Skillan hardly knew what to make of the decayed yet peripatetic Lodovico, and I for one did not blame him.

The stage-pictures were very fine, and the Cardinal's robe was as a cascade of blood from the Websterian fount.

*October* 12.

# Foreign Plays and Adaptations

.

# "Six Characters in Search of an Author"

A COMEDY BY LUIGI PIRANDELLO

# "Henry IV"

A TRAGEDY BY LUIGI PIRANDELLO
NEW OXFORD THEATRE

# "Henry IV"

ENGLISH VERSION
EVERYMAN THEATRE

# "And That's the Truth"

A COMEDY BY LUIGI PIRANDELLO
LYRIC THEATRE, HAMMERSMITH

THIS week has been for me a defeat, if not a complete rout. I do not know, alas, a single word of Italian, and to sit stone-deaf before two plays, every word of which is an intellectual challenge, induces in me maximum exasperation. It is like taking a

45

picture-lover into a gallery, blindfolding him, and bidding him judge a Cézanne by his finger-tips. All that follows here, then, is a hodge-podge of the printed page and the visible, entirely unintelligible superficies of the plays in performance. Add the lesson taught by the early critics of Ibsen and Shaw, unlearned as yet by the detractors of Tchehov and Glaspell, and the reader must see how pathetically anxious I am not to be mistaken in Pirandello. At the same time I will never be bluffed into deeming any play " marvellous," in Mr. Coward's lingo, simply because I cannot understand it.

These things being said, let me suggest that I find Pirandello to be a great dramatist for those very reasons which the Pirandellists deny. They insist that the master has broken the bounds set to the old-fashioned " sentimental " Latin play, and abandoned those largely ethical motivations of the " old " theatre which developed spiritual crises from the conflict of impulses with a rigid framework of law and convention. What, then, has Pirandello substituted ? Simply the theory of Relativity as applied to persons instead of to formulæ. I confess that this seems to be not very new. The idea that two people, having a different sense and value of things, can never really communicate is sufficiently familiar. To me a person whose soul is centred in the acquisition of used, or even unused, postage-stamps is demented ; to your fresh-air fiend a man who for pleasure spends a fine summer evening mewed up in a stuffy theatre is obviously a lunatic. How can the words " good " and " bad " have any meaning between people who have such different standards of what is desirable and undesirable ? It is only a step from this to the imperfect differentiation between sane and insane, real and unreal.

Are characters in a book real ? An English poet has written of those legendary heroes " who soon as we are born are straight our friends." Is not Mr. Micawber the friend of every Englishman from the day of his birth ? Is he less *real* than the thousands of actual people who, once seen, are never remembered ? Would Mr. Micawber have existed if Dickens, dissatisfied with his novel, had never given it to the press ? That's the whole burden of *Six Characters in Search of an Author*. The Pirandellists are particularly anxious that we should look upon these works as stage-dramas and not as philosophical dissertations. I humbly suggest that in the theatre the comedy, if not the tragedy, comes off excellently. First you have the stage filled with a company of actors complete with manager, prompter, and stage hands. Could any collection of people be more real ? We think no, and are immediately confuted. For the Six Characters, never quite brought to birth by their author and " side-tracked " by him, now appear, looking not so much like the unborn as the recently-interred. And at once they put up a show of living, the fierce intensity of which makes ghosts of the real people on the stage. Perhaps the most stupid objection to Matisse, Picasso and their kind is that they can't draw, the only possible semblance of a real point being that they won't, preferring to do something else. It jumps to the eyes in this comedy that if Pirandello cared to write a straightforward play he would have no superior living. The reaction of these Six Characters among themselves is magnificent drama, though no more tortured way of presenting it could be imagined. It is their story—belonging incidentally to the old " sentimental " theatre as defined above—which interests us, though the main theme of the play is their superiority to the flesh-and-blood actors. Yet one would not dogmatise. No moment in the terrible story of the Father and the Step-daughter has quite so much " theatre " in it as the evocation of Madame Pace—who is Mr. Shaw's Mrs. Warren—by the reconstitution of the material surroundings in which she carried on her nefarious trade.

Frankly, of " Henry IV " in cold print I could make nothing at all. Let not the Pirandellists rage too furiously together ; I speak for myself, not for them. Of the play in the theatre I made something, but only for such periods as the King was on the stage. When he was absent—for immense periods, alas !—the play seemed to me to be one long wilderness of dementia. Large tracts of it were concerned with the re-incarnation of a mother in her daughter—a theme which both Maupassant and our own Hardy have handled with tragic pity. But I do not believe anybody in the theatre could have told me whether, at any particular moment, the mother was speaking in her own person, or in that of her former self, or as the embodiment of the eleventh-century Marchioness she had impersonated. The Marchioness, in other words, obscured the drama—"an obstacle that came between," as Lewis Carroll might have put it, " her and ourselves and it." But the madness was the thing. Henry's diseasèd brain was like those calceolarias invented by Des Esseintes to resemble tumours, and glowed with a colour and energy denied to healthy blooms. And just as the Six Characters were more alive than the real people, so Henry's mind, working in terms of an unknown reason, was obviously made of more perceptive stuff than that in which our more familiar logic works. Henry's lucidity, like Lear's, shone most when his mind was what we should call darkest, for we must remember that mad people ratiocinate intensively within the circle of their own reason, though that reason is not ours. Henry's intellectuality was such that when sanity overcame him he still towered above his court like genius among valetry. If only Pirandello would abandon those wretched metaphysics ! But I suppose you might as well ask Cubist painters to draw cows which look like cows. That's not what they're after : and Pirandello was certainly not after writing a simple tragedy like *Hamlet*, which any fellow can understand.

Are we, I wonder, in for a wave of portentous abstraction ? As I write, an American magazine comes tumbling from the skies containing a story by Maxim Gorky. It is about a woman who meets a novelist and "adopts a cautious attitude towards him." He is a man *who does not exist*, and though his physical

49

self is present his soul, however attractive it seems to be, is absent ! The woman goes for a walk and meets a character out of her friend's novel. The character has been deserted by his wife, and does not know whether he is supposed to meet her again, the rest of his story not being written. This shadowy personage, the unnatural movements of whose body remind the woman of a sheet shaken in a breeze, then soliloquises : " One sits and thinks : how boring, how foolish and prolix real people can be, and how much more interesting we imaginary creations are ! We are always more spiritually concentrated, we have more poetry and romance about us. And to think that we exist solely for the amusement of these dull real people ! " Will the Pirandellists forgive me if I " adopt a cautious attitude " towards their idol's plays, and if I draw a parallel between the master's concern for his precious metaphysics and Wagner's craze for philosophic theory ?

Ruggero Ruggeri is a really fine tragic actor, possessing all that Barrymore owns together with all which that actor lacks, and Marta Abba shows herself to be of the stuff of which Duses are made.

*June* 15, 18.

Of all people in the world your high-brow is the easiest to take in. A foreign author, baggy-trousered auspices, half-a-dozen undergraduates disposed about the stage like the lovesick maidens in *Patience,* an entirely unintelligible plot—and he falls for the thing

at once. " The dust of an earthy to-day is the earth
of a dusty to-morrow," says Signor Pirandello, or words
to that effect ; and the high-brow concatenation
shrieks out the " Too perfectly marvellous ! " which is
to-day's equivalent of the eighties' " Too utterly
utter ! " Let me, emerging from Hampstead's tulgy
heath, draw an honest, vorpal blade, and declare that
*Henry IV* is pretentious nonsense, and that the high-
brow frenzy for it is largely composed of the feeling
that not to enthuse is to be out of the fashionable swim.

Only the other day my wise and witty colleague, Mr.
Ernest Newman, was telling us that if one man says
that Yankee Doodle is a good tune, and another man says
that it isn't, there is really no use in going on with the
discussion. All you can do with a tune is to sing it over
again. But you can go some way towards deciding
whether a play is a good one or not by paraphrasing it.
A. is persuaded by Mrs. A. to murder their host B. If
B. is a king, then Mr. and Mrs. A. bag his kingdom ;
if a private individual, they collar the insurance money.
The happiness of the A.s is complete except for B.'s ghost,
and their own consciences. The tragedy lies largely
in the fact that A. is a poet and Mrs. A. a loving wife
and capable " manager." Yes, *Macbeth* in the baldest
paraphrase is obviously a good play. Now let us do the
same thing for *Henry IV*. X. twenty years ago was
kicked on the head by his horse, and has been potty ever
since. Potty, that is, according to the standards of
people who have not been kicked on the head by a
horse. X.'s madness induces him to believe that he is

still the eleventh-century monarch impersonated by him in the pageant at the time of the accident. He recovers his wits for a space, and proceeds to round upon his keepers, who have decently humoured him when they might have clapped him into a strait-jacket. In a pet he commits murder, and then to save his neck has to pretend that he is still mad. But he has already decided that a life of pretended insanity is better than other people's sanity.

It is not the question of madness or non-madness that I find worrying. It is possible that the moon may be made of green cheese, that the earth is flat, that men and trees and houses are holes in the solid ether, that the whole universe is but a corpuscle in the blood of a gnat, that a smile may exist without a Cheshire cat to support it. I am perfectly willing that a play should take all these suppositions for a working hypothesis. What is worrying is that I find it impossible to care whether this pretended Henry IV is mad or not. "Oh, what a noble mind is here o'er-thrown" was said of Hamlet, whom to know is to love. Is there anything lovable about the Italian hero? Is there anything human, as there is about the Macbeths? Do we care whether he lives or dies? Take that speech to his valets :—

> Do you think it's a joke that the dead continue to live . . . But get out into the live world ! Ah, you say ; what a beautiful sunrise—for us ! All time is before us !—Dawn ! We will do what we like with this day——. Ah, yes ! To Hell with tradition, the old conventions ! Well,

go on ! You will do nothing but repeat the old,
old words, while you imagine you are living !

Then consider his proposals as to how these young
men might more usefully employ their lives :—

> I say that—you are fools ! You ought to
> have known how to create a fantasy for yourselves,
> naturally, simply, day by day, before nobody,
> feeling yourselves alive in the history of the
> eleventh century. . . . You would have drunk it
> in with the air you breathed, yet knowing all the
> time that it was a dream, so you could better enjoy
> the privilege afforded you of having to do nothing
> else but live this dream, this far-off and yet actual
> dream. And to think that at a distance of eight
> centuries from this remote age of ours, so coloured
> and so sepulchral, the men of the twentieth century
> are torturing themselves in ceaseless anxiety to
> know how their fates and fortunes will work out.
> Whereas you are already in history with me. . . .

To reject life for the sake of a mouldy dream seems to
me to be the very poison of decadence. To plead that
the man is mad is no excuse. Hamlet did not urge us
to drink up Eisel or eat crocodiles. Every word
uttered by Henry is pessimistic to the point of corruption. And therefore I deem the play evil. There
is not in it, I maintain, one single shred of ordinary,
decent, human feeling. " What is there then to arouse
so much enthusiasm ? " I asked one frantic Pirandellist.
He replied : " Well, I like the different angles from
which the problem of reality is surveyed. I like the
grouping, I like the stage-patterns, the gestures, and

attitudes of the actors. I like Mr. Milton's bedroom slippers. Of course, there is no human interest, but I like the visible surface of the thing. I like it as ballet. I should like it just as well if it were in Chinese."

" But it is in Chinese," I murmured.

Let me suggest that Signor Pirandello has hoodwinked my friend by his amazing faculty for presentation. This dramatist possesses a technical equipment as elaborate as that of Ibsen, Labiche, or our own Pinero ; and he uses his wonderful craftsmanship to conceal the fact that he has nothing whatever to say. Nothing, that is, outside the realm of metaphysical speculation. The madman will hold out his arm, feel his wrist, and exclaim " Sometimes I am even afraid of my own blood pulsing loudly in my arteries in the silence of night, like the sound of a distant step in a lonely corridor." Here the world seems to stand still for the utterance. But there's nothing in it beyond the glib, deft gesture. Next moment he is off on some nonsense about living his madness with the most lucid consciousness ; he would revenge himself on the brutality of the stone which has dinted his head. And so on and so forth. There is no thought in this play, only the elaborately fashioned shell of thinking.

No good actor can fail to be impressive who is allowed to sail the limelight in a white wig, sackcloth, and felt slippers, and who has the Larger Lunacy to draw upon for words. The Pirandellists signified by their applause that, in their view, Mr. Ernest Milton had given a fine performance. I shall not be so impertinent as to offer an opinion upon this clever actor's interpretation of that which I deem to be plain gibberish. There was one piece of acting which excited my complete admiration, and that was Mr. Geoffrey Wincott's Berthold. This young man was ordained to shrink against the wainscotting throughout the whole piece in complete and total bewilderment at every word uttered. This the actor realised quite perfectly.

*July* 16.

> I remember once being driven in a hansom cab down a street that turned out to be a *cul de sac*, and brought us bang up against a wall. The driver and I simultaneously said something. But I said: " That'll never do ! " and the cabman said, " This is all right ! "—G. K. CHESTERTON.

Was there ever bonnet-bee of such buzz and persistency as that which afflicts poor Signor Pirandello ? The hum of this insect was the ground bass to Thursday night's proceedings at Hammersmith, and the high-brow audience reciprocated with the whirr of brains in maximum cerebration. The house applauded systematically as each favourite in Mr. Playfair's team made entrance or exit, and altogether it was a noisy evening. But I venture to say, with enormous diffidence, that I have not the least intention of being bounced into liking a play which I regard as inherently wrong from beginning to end.

There's nothing either good or bad but thinking makes it so, is a self-evident proposition. There has never been pretence that " good " and " bad " are anything but expressions of opinion. And human opinion, too. That it is good for men to eat beef is accepted by most of us, but not, one imagines, by the oxen. That it is lawful to snap up human beings is a view held by sharks and contradicted by Polynesian natives. Man finds tobacco-smoke delightful, whereas the greenfly holds it to be obnoxious, and holds this opinion so strongly that it makes no bones about dying for it. It all depends upon the point of view. And now comes Signor Pirandello, who would have it that there's nothing true or untrue, but thinking makes it so. Here is the snag which our intellectuals will not perceive.

Take three persons, A, B, and C. A is kind to B and unkind to C. A, then, in B's opinion, must be a kind man, in C's an unkind one. But cannot our relativists see that A's make-up contains both kindness and cruelty, and that the measure of these two ingredients is in no way determined by the incomplete knowledge of them held by B and C? Kindness and cruelty, charity and meanness, and a thousand other qualities— what we call A's character—cannot be perfectly known to anybody except himself, and may even not be known by him. But it exists, absolute at any moment yet with all its potentialities of change, and at all times in the old devout phrase " known unto God." " They say the owl was a baker's daughter," moaned wandering Ophelia. But is not it obvious that the owl's paternity was definite, and independent of whatever the baker may have thought about it? What Signor Pirandello will not see is that Relativity is concerned only with the happiness or unhappiness of the baker according to the view he holds of the matter. The present play is made to hang upon the recognition or denial of the fact that one person cannot be himself and somebody else at the same time. Signor Pirandello neither confirms nor denies this ; he says you can think what you like about it. Which is nonsense.

Signor Ponza has immured his wife, and allows her mother, Signora Frola, to converse with her from a distance only. Provincial Italian society is anxious to know why this should be. Signora Frola's version is as follows : The immured Signora Ponza is really her daughter who, some years earlier, fell ill. This illness so distressed Ponza that he was sent to an asylum. The wife recovered, but Ponza remained mad in so far as he maintained that his wife was dead, and remarried her in the belief that she was another woman. To humour him, Signora Frola pretends that she is a lunatic who mistakes the second wife for her own dead daughter. Ponza's story, on the other hand, is that his first wife did actually die, and that it is his mother in-law who is out of her mind. He, in his turn, confesses to pretended madness out of regard for the other. These are the statements of the first act.

The second act poses the question : which of the two is a lunatic ? They are confronted, and their real and simulated derangements at once set up multiple reflections like opposing mirrors. In the third act the bright idea occurs to somebody : Why not send for the

57

wife and let her declare who she is ? The suggestion is thrown out that Signora Ponza may be a Mrs. Harris, that Ponza is living with the ghost of a memory and Signora Frola cherishing a phantom regret. For we are to mark that nobody has seen the woman, and that the whole argument up to now has been based on the lines of Mr. Justice Stareleigh's famous summing-up. If Signora Bardell-Frola is right, it is perfectly clear that Signor Pickwick-Ponza is wrong, and if the audience-jury think the evidence of Signora Cluppins worthy of credence they will believe it, and, if they don't, why they won't. So the vital witness comes in to settle the matter, and when she appears veiled we know that our worst suspicions are confirmed. At once she declares herself to be either the first wife or the second, or both together, or anything anybody likes. The audience has paid its half-guinea and is at liberty to make its own choice.

Signor Pirandello has tacked Relativity on to a matter which cannot possibly be subject to Relativity. The dramatic significance in this play should lie not at all in the question of identity—which is what we are made to pursue throughout the whole evening—but in the influence upon the husband and mother-in-law of their views as to that identity. Is it better to be sane and lose a cherished object, or mad and keep it ? This is the true drama, whereas the poser which Signor Pirandello prefers is whether we take the object to be teacup or teacaddy. Relativity is Signor Pirandello's bane ; a few precious people may hold it to be his

virtue, but precious few will agree with them.   Relativity has, in my judgment, entirely ruined every play
of his that I have seen, for the simple reason that it has
led him to use a magnificent technical equipment to
dethrone that human interest which in the theatre
should be paramount.   What is moving in *Six Characters* is not whether these unborn creatures may be said
to exist, but the tragedy which they want to tell us.
What interests me in the present play is the " story "
behind grief of such momentum that its impact destroys
reason.   But that is the tale Signor Pirandello will not
tell, preferring that we should spend the evening guess-
ing which of two lunatics is the likelier.

The piece was admirably acted.   Mr. Playfair contributed a masterpiece of *aplomb*, Mr. Claude Rains
one of virtuosity, and Mr. Guy Lefeuvre one of finick-
ing meddlesomeness.   Miss Nancy Price gave a good
study of a withered beldam, half harpy and half crone,
with some moments of pathos.   Miss Dorothy Green's
five minutes at the end snatched up the piece into those
regions wherein it was highly, if wrongly, conceived.

*September* 17.

# " Peer Gynt "

## By HENRIK IBSEN

## O. U. D. S.

IT must be a fine thing to be young and at Oxford, to wear pull-overs more gorgeous than the necks of pheasants, to proclaim flaming hopes of a Theatre of Ideas in which the world's masterpieces shall be constantly revived. Let me not dash youth's ardour by suggesting that this country knows no such theatre. After all, the peculiar virtue of hope lies in the hoping, not in the realisation.

Writing in 1896 of the performance of Ibsen's philosophic poem at the Théâtre de L'Œuvre, Mr. Shaw predicted an English vogue round about 1920. He was more or less right about the date, and more or less wrong about the vogue. Rapture at the " Old Vic " spells something very different across the river. To affirm that the Boyg, the Button-Moulder, and the Strange Passenger would in our time—or, indeed, in any time—become as familiar to the English people as Shakespeare's Witches or Goethe's Mephistopheles— this was just Mr. Shaw's youthful nonsense. Your average English playgoer takes to the Witches in

*Macbeth* because he is not compelled to think about them, and can simply accept them as part of the scenery, like the battlements at Elsinore ; and it may be doubted whether he knows sufficient of Goethe's Mephistopheles to climb into the saddle of cogitation, Gounod's familiar personage being a horse of an entirely different colour.  But the whole point about Ibsen's queer fish is that you must think about them.  In the way of concrete, self-sufficing drama, standing tub-like on its own bottom—such drama as Hamlet's stabbing of the arras and his cry, " Is it the King ? "—these rum folk don't bear thinking about.  Or, put it the other way round, and say that it is only by thinking about them that they can be made bearable.  Now, thinking in the theatre may be fairly good meat for the Norwegians ; it is still, whatever Mr. Shaw may say, pretty average poison for audiences assembling west of Waterloo.

The truth of the matter is that *Peer Gynt*, like *Faust*, falls into two parts, the second of which can never be intelligible unless it is acted in its entirety.  The first half is as mother's milk—none can be so poor of imagination as not to behold his own boyhood in this shaggy Norwegian Hamlet.  Ase's death is one of the most grandly inspired things in all romantic drama.  The boy astride his chair, driving his mother hell-for-leather to the gates of Heaven, and all to the honour and glory of his wild, poetic, impossibly romantic self—this is a conception not above, nor below, but outside Shakespeare, and worthy to rank with the most poignant of *Lear*.

61

How great a poet Ibsen is in his own language I have no means of knowing, but even in translation the closing passage of this scene attains to marvellous beauty. Peer, his frenzy over, and closing his mother's eyes, has this requiem :

> For all of your days I thank you,
> For beatings and lullabys !

Here he kisses the dead face.

> But see, you must thank me back, now—
> There ; that was the driver's fare.

In its place, on the stage, there is nothing in all Shakespeare to shame " beatings and lullabys."

And since comparisons are going, then

> Saint Peter ! you're in for it now !
> Have done with these jack-in-office airs, sir !

might be likened to the voice of Browning.

Up to Ase's death there is nothing which the most intrepid producer can cut, except, perhaps, about half of everything everybody has to say, and all the queer political allusions. No bulk excisions are possible. But two hours have passed, and less than two remain for all those diffuse yet reinforcing experiences of Peer's later life. Forty years of greed, vanity, egotism, braggadocio, heartlessness, sentimentality, courage, cowardice—each quality a facet of Gyntism, a way of " being oneself "—if Ibsen could not get this into two hours it is certain that his abbreviators can't. What, then, is the proper thing to do ? The obvious

thing, one says hastily, is to cut all such irrelevances as
gibes at the King of Sweden, and the note-mongering
habit of Norwegian and Swedish officials. But the
matter isn't as easy as all that. The scene in the mad-
house, in which these apparent excrescences occur, is
one of the most exciting in the whole play. The
Fellah with the mummy on his back, the Pen which
insists upon cutting itself, Peer's terror, his collapse
and ironic coronation—all this is great drama to the
eye, though it is not until Begriffenfeldt gives the
shout " Long Life to Self-hood's Kaiser ! " that
we can " connect " with the central self-realisation
*motif*.

All honour to Mr. Reginald Denham that he
retained this mad-house scene. Incidentally, the
staging and grouping here were both expressionist and
admirable. (Perhaps Huhu, who is no more than a
skit on language-reformers, might have been omitted.)
All honour to Mr. Denham, and his advisers, if any,
that he retained the exquisite speech of the Pastor
speaking beside the grave. Perhaps there was not
quite enough insistence on Peer's smug reflection that
he, too, is just such another simple hero as the dead
man, who was, in fact, precisely his opposite in character. But amends were made in the onion scene,
showing man to be all layers and no core—" Nature is
so witty." We were not to have the " pig " speech,
but we got most of the boat. Among the lost treasures
was the scene in the water after the shipwreck, where
Peer half drowns the Cook and then holds him up by

the hair so that he may mumble the, at that moment, irrelevant petition for daily bread. But we had the Strange Passenger's second appearance, and the whole meaning of the play was driven home by a full-length presentation of the Button-Moulder.

I am not sure that any producer, however skilful, can prevent the audience from interpreting Solveig's last consolatory appearance as the conventional Lyceum apotheosis of Redemption by Love. This is Peer's view of the situation which Ibsen is at such pains to deny. Demolition ought to come in the Button-Moulder's cackling threat that they will meet again at the last cross-road, "and *then* we'll see whether . . ." His voice trails away. What is to be seen at the last cross-road is whether a good woman's love can redeem a weak man's paltriness. But that is in the future, whereas what the audience sees is Peer preparing to take his flight into Abraham's bosom *viá* that of Solveig. And this ending is too comfortable and too little disconcerting not to be eagerly accepted by the sentimental. Yes, the fault is certainly Ibsen's.

At Oxford all the armoury of intelligence was used to keep this second part together. And yet the attempt failed, as it always must. One felt as if one were at the heart of meaning though unpossessed of its easier, more negotiable fringe. Thus a voyager lost in the bowels of a ship among the engines, and anxious to get his head above deck with a chance of asking the captain where he is making for. But Ibsen was never your man for a plain answer to a plain question, though he

delighted in making a pet point some dozen or score
of times. How tired we got at Oxford of those
repeated expositions of the true meaning of " being oneself " ! And perhaps we didn't very greatly care how
soon the middle-aged Peer ceased to be himself or anybody else ! Peer in tattered shirt and with tousled hair
is one thing : Peer in a caftan and, later, an abominable
plaid deer-stalker, ear-flaps and all, is another. His
tragedy is spiritual and profound, but it isn't visually
too entertaining, and perhaps Mr. Kipling put it all
rather more amusing in *Tomlinson*. And the Button-
Moulder, what a bore ! Vital though he is, and the
most important person in the piece after Peer, he
becomes an intolerable nuisance round about half-past
eleven. How he harps on the same worn string !
How must he chop infantile logic with himself so that
it sounds like an imaginary conversation between the
authors of *Donovan* and *Robert Elsmere*. If there is
any more tedious character in the play I should plump
for Peer himself in his salacious moods. A clammy,
cold mist has been declared by one great critic to
enwrap Ibsen's sensuousness. " The people cry up
the roses and raptures of Swinburnian ethics in tones
that would freeze a faun and send a Bacchante to the
nearest Methodist chapel in search of doctrine less
shiversome." I agree. Peer as a middle-aged roué
is unutterably depressing. *Read* Peer's tragedy, and
you still see the fascinating boy in the maundering,
mouthing compromise for a man. But see him on the
stage fingering a greying beard, shaking the ponderous

flaps of that awful deer-stalker, and leaning heavily on his umbrella, and you reflect first that the eyes of the mind and the eyes of the body are two different things, and second that the early caricaturists and parodists of Ibsen were not frightfully wide of the mark.

Mr. R. W. Speaight gave an excellent performance of the youthful Peer. The impetuosity, the vanity, the adventure, the *excitement* of living were all admirably suggested. The prating boy's imagination was on fire, and that of the audience was soon sympathetically alight. The young actor's voice and gestures were extremely good ; there was subtlety and modulation in both. If there was a fault here it was that Peer was too lovable. He lacked the uncouth husk, the gnarled ferocity which made him disliked of all his world. In the later scenes, which demanded the momentum of a much older player, Mr. Speaight was not very successful, and indeed could not hope to be. He was obviously a boy who had surrendered cranium and chin to the artifices of the admirable Mr. Willie Clarkson. But there is more than wiggery in the elder Peer. Mr. A. Tandy gave the Parson's long speech most beautifully, and if Mr. Gyles Isham (last year's Hamlet) thought he could cloak his fine delivery under a pseudonym and the mask of the Strange Passenger he was mistaken. Messrs. A. E. Franklin, J. H. James, J. Maud, L. Nye, and particularly H. Grisewood (the Button-Moulder) must be singled out for special praise. Miss Clare Greet was very moving throughout Ase's dying, and, realising that the scene is really Peer's, she

66

was content like the great artist she is to subordinate her share. Miss Joan Maude as Solveig looked and spoke prettily, and Miss Eva Albanesi's Anitra was pleasant. A large orchestra acquitted itself nobly under Dr. W. H. Harris, and the occasion was a great one, even for Oxford.

Let me end by repeating my admiration for Mr. Denham's producing. The lighting throughout was admirable, and so was the drilling. You could not have guessed that the cast were nearly all amateurs.

*February* 10.

# " A Doll's House "

## By HENRIK IBSEN

### The Playhouse

MISS MADGE TITHERADGE has very greatly advanced her reputation by her successful excursion into Ibsen and really fine playing of Nora. Or perhaps one would say that she has at one blow launched a new reputation in the theatrical world. Hitherto one has regarded this actress as being a superb mistress in the art of making fascinating bricks out of inconceivably dull straw, of giving point to the pointless and some show of sincerity to the insincere. If a part was limp and lifeless the producer would send for Miss Titheradge to vitalise it, or galvanise it into some semblance of life. In other words, one went to the theatre to see the player rather than the play. But redemptive work of this nature carries with it its own penalties. The actress, having no character in which to sink herself, is thrown entirely upon the exploitation of her own personality, so that winsome little mole-hills of manner become mountains of artificiality. It must be confessed that Miss Titheradge had not entirely escaped this said forfeit. Then came that very notable first performance of Nora in *A Doll's House*, and at once a new and entirely different artist stepped upon the stage. Every vestige of artificiality had disappeared, and one was conscious that it was Nora, and not Miss Titheradge, who was fibbing, and hanging herself round Torvald's neck, and eating the macaroons.

Without following Miss Titheradge all the way through the piece, let me say that this was the best acting of Nora that I have ever seen. The doll-like heroine retained her doll-quality even after the shock of awakening at the end. Many Noras make the mistake of growing up suddenly into full stature and giving one the impression that they are ready not only to march out into the night but to chain themselves to the gates of St. Stephen's and harangue the policeman on duty. Too many Noras make for themselves an ultimate head of Gorgon or Medusa wherewith to petrify the unfortunate Torvald, who now finds that he has cherished in his bosom a highly intelligent snake instead of a silly dove. One of the points about this play is that Nora at the end really does believe that she has acted throughout like a silly little ninny with nonsensical ideas about self-sacrifice, and that her children will be contaminated by her folly and ignorance. Most Noras slam the door in Torvald's face with the spiteful air of one wishing to catch his nose in the jamb; Miss Titheradge closes it after her gently, because it is the proper thing to do whether you are leaving a room, a house, or an old life.

Time does, indeed, bring the most preposterous

changes. This early play of Ibsen—it was written in 1878—aroused in the beginning the most violent controversies. It was all very well, people said, for Nora to awake to a sense of her own individuality, and responsibility to that individuality. But wasn't the desertion of the children carrying egotism a trifle too far, since that pretence of not being a fit companion for them was always a bit too thin? Sequels to the play were written. Sir Walter Besant wrote one, which Mr. Shaw, then in the first flush of intoxicated Ibsenism, capped by following this sequel by yet another sequel. In those days Womanly Woman was still the great ideal. " In India," says Mr. Shaw, " they carried this piece of idealism to the length of declaring that a wife could not bear to survive her husband, but would be prompted by her own faithful, loving, beautiful nature to offer up her life on the pyre which consumed his dead body. The astonishing thing is that women, sooner than be branded as unsexed wretches, allowed themselves to be stupefied with drink, and in that unwomanly condition burnt alive. British Philistinism put down widow-idealising with a strong hand ; and suttee is abolished in India." Ibsen's play was really meant to put an end to wife-idealising. We begin to feel now, I think, that Nora's departure was never very much more than a gesture, and, in any case, we have ceased to inquire what became of her afterwards. There is a sense in which revolt is in itself a sufficient end. It can be a protest against the unbearable, and whether what follows is still more unbearable is really beside the point. The revolt has to be made just as Nora has to slam that door. Forty years ago the play annoyed everybody intensely. There could be no possible justification, it was said, for any wife to desert any husband. Whereupon Ibsen promptly wrote *Ghosts*, which shows the awful mess which may result when a wife cannot be induced to desert some particular husband. Which, in its turn, raised an uproar rather bigger than the preceding one. But Ibsen was like that, and we can see the cantankerous old fellow rubbing his hands in glee.

And now time has brought its revenges. *A Doll's House* is "too old-fashioned, my dear, for anything." There is no longer any sex war except in the purely material question as to whether some women should be engaged to do a man's work rather better than some men can do it and for a good deal less pay. One does not believe that a performance of Nora by plain, unknown Miss Biffkins, of Balham, supposing it to have been quite as good as that by the beautiful and famous Miss Titheradge, would have excited the smallest attention. The truth about that brilliant first night at the Playhouse is that the audience went to see an adorable and fascinating artist, in spite of the fact that she was to appear in a world-masterpiece. And very much to their astonishment they saw not Miss Titheradge magnoperating as Miss Titheradge, but very humbly, conscientiously, and sincerely acting and being Nora.

The rest of the cast supported her nobly, though at least one member of it added to Miss Titheradge's responsibilities by relying upon her in the *rôle* of prompter. Mr. Milton Rosmer has probably learnt his part by now, though he made us often feel very uncomfortable during the first two acts. But when once he got into his stride he was very good indeed, and the scenes of befuddlement and denunciation were admirable. Too many Helmers make the mistake of resembling Uriah Heep. Mr. Rosmer's husband was entirely plausible, and one felt that Nora really could have lived with him without finding him out. I liked Mr. Harcourt Williams's Doctor Rank, who might, however, have been a trifle gloomier. One had the feeling that he was not really more than off colour, and that a month at St. Andrews would put him all right again. The Mrs. Linden of Miss Martita Hunt was the best I have ever seen, and Nils Krogstad was played by Mr. Frederick Lloyd conscientiously, if with little inspiration.

*December 2.*

# "The Wild Duck"

## A Play by Henrik Ibsen

### St. James's Theatre

THIS play, if only you leave the wild duck out of it, is a good deal plainer than any pikestaff I have ever seen. It is as plain as the nose on anybody else's face, only you must not shut your eyes to it. You must not say : " I do not like snub noses. All plays about snub noses are bad plays. This play is about a nose that is distinctly *retroussé*. Therefore, this play is a bad play."

How it would have warmed the cockles of Ibsen's heart—presuming that frigid organ to have had any cockles—to have been present on Wednesday night at the St. James's Theatre and note how every thrust and every sally went home to an ordinary, middling-brow audience ! Why, one asks oneself, should there ever have been doubt as to the drift of the play's extraordinarily lucid argument, or the meaning of its total gesture ? What, apart from the duck herself, can the bogey have been ? Let us admit that that fearful wild-fowl and eponymous heroine has always been something of a difficulty, and remains so still. Who is it, besides herself, that in this play dives down into the ocean-depths and bites fast hold of the weed, wrack, and all the rubbish down there? Gregers, we know, tries to fasten the symbol upon Hjalmar Ekdal, likening himself to the clever dog who goes down after the wounded bird and rescues her. But there is nothing of the wild duck about the photographer, who is nothing but the most ordinary domestic gander, mistaking himself for one of life's swans. Is she Hedvig, the child who sacrifices herself for her father, or the old sportsman Ekdal, or is the poor fowl not anybody at all but the spirit of Truth, Sacrifice, or any other of the abstract Virtues?

All sorts of theories have been held about this piece. The older critics, from Brandes to William Archer, held that in it Ibsen, disappointed at the reception of *Ghosts*, turned and rent his own ideals like the man who bites his finger to allay a hurt elsewhere. Or, again, Ibsen might possibly be deemed to turn upon his public with some such savage cry as : " I tried to show you how much good facing the facts about marriage would have done the Alvings. You wouldn't have that. Here I show you how much harm came to the Ekdals by having the facts about their marriage thrust upon them by a meddlesome idealist. Let's see if you like that any better."

But is not the play quite easy if we disregard the petty, spiteful consideration, and look squarely upon it as standing by itself, isolated, yet a link in the chain of Ibsen's thought like a peak in a mountain range? Is it not possible that, for once in a way, the vaunted symbolism just did not come off? Leave the duck out of it, close that garret door, and the piece is perfectly plain·

The whole point is obviously the mischief wrought, not by truth, but by the indiscreet use of truth. Gregers, by his gluttony for an idealism which he can only half digest, shows us first that one of the effects of thrusting your finger into a pie may be to ruin it, and second, that the proper people to conduct that operation are the owners of the pie. No attack is made upon the sanctity of marriage : wrath and ridicule are poured upon the husband, whose mind is so entirely eaten away by false pretence, folly, and indulgence in sham sentiment that it simply cannot entertain a sane thought about anything in the world, sacred or profane. This play is bound up with all the others in this—that the beneficence of an ideal depends not upon the ideal, but upon the fitness to receive it of the person upon whom it is thrust. Is he ready for it ? If so, then the thrust may be expected to come from within. The play is really an attack upon meddlers.

It is not to be thought that the acted play is anything like as serious as the analysis of it must be. The whole of the action is centred in the preposterous carryings-on of the farcical photographer. He is glorious fun, and the audience at the St. James's laughed long and loud enough to make nervous wrecks of themselves for weeks. Mr. Milton Rosmer, made up to look like young Beethoven, poured out Ekdal like a glass of beer, toasted our sense of fun, and blew the froth in our faces. It was a capital, racy performance. Possibly there might have been a trifle more exaltation about the Gregers Werle of Mr. Ion Swinley, made up to look like young Matthew Arnold, but also looking and talking rather like one of those ineffectual tub-thumpers whose audience has dwindled to two ragged little girls and a baby in arms. But within the limitations of personality the performance was good, and there was no gainsaying its intelligence.

As Old Ekdal, Mr. Brember Wills put on the full armour of Ibsenite senility, and, attired in the panoply of his old shako, and somebody else's stable jacket, presented the kind of figure whom William Blake would have asked to tea. Anything more terrifying than the jut of that right brow overhanging that cavernous right eye, while the left interrogated the heaven with the despondent glare of a moulting vulture —anything fuller of awe than this I do not remember. As Hedvig Miss Angela Baddeley acted astonishingly well, breaking down in one place only when, after one of the most lacerating storms of childish weeping I ever remember, she lifted her head from the horsehair sofa and revealed a countenance innocent of all emotion. It may be that the films and the geyser-like Gish family have vitiated taste to the extent of making us demand real tears. I leave this to the actress, but somehow or other she must get agony into her countenance corresponding to her weeping. But the rest of the part was played in an entirely lovely manner. Gina was acted cosily and comfortably by Miss Sybil Arundale, and the rest of the cast was quite good. The setting and dresses of 1884 were admirable.

*July* 15.

76

# " The Cherry Orchard "

## A Play by ANTON TCHEHOV

### Lyric, Hammersmith

Ah ! insensé qui crois que tu n'es pas moi.—Victor Hugo.

INSULARITY is a good thing, perhaps, but not always as we islanders conceive it. " These Russians have a very un-English way of looking at things," I heard a lady say at the conclusion of this piece. That's our trouble. " If people are not English, they ought to be," puts our view in a nutshell. Tchehov's characters maunder and drivel, barren equally of purpose and that last refuge of the shiftless— optimism. There is no " drive " about them ; they do not " get a move on " ; they potter about, Micawbers for whom there is not even a Port Middle- bay. Dickens could not refuse his magnanimous shirker a shadowy success, even if it had to be of the antipodean sort. Tchehov makes no such pretence ; his " job-lots " are doomed from the beginning.

Mr. Shaw's Britannus was a barbarian who thought that the customs of his tribe and island were the laws of nature. In judging this play we must not be Britannús. It is possible that in Russian eyes Micawber,

77

my uncle Toby, even Falstaff himself are no more than mindless buffoons. Let us beware of rating Tchehov's company as passive mug-wumps, and refrain from annoyance that they will not *exuberate*, to use Johnson's word, into doers and contrivers. I make this plea purely on behalf of those who must put a work of art to the test of reason rather than emotion. *The Cherry Orchard* is really like one of those pictures in which Utrillo invites you to look at a tenement-dwelling in Montmartre. He does not argue that the house is unsanitary, that it shelters crime and vice, that it should be pulled down. He just paints it. You may not want to live in such a house, but its presentment gives you pleasure. Tchehov too presents, without condemning, his *fainéants*. You would not live with them in the flesh ? Try living with them in the spirit.

Which of these portraits do we like best ? Is it that of Leonid Gayef, the sieve of sentiment, who will pour out his soul to an old cupboard and almost frighten you with his obsession of billiards ? Have we not all some *trac* indifferently mastered ? Or do we prefer Trophimof, that pathetic student who dislikes solemnity and takes himself with immense seriousness ? Or Lopahkin, the successful man, who won't, we feel, really make money out of the villas he is to build on the site of the cherry orchard ? Or Pishtchik, the fat, jovial sponger, who has had two strokes, takes other people's pills, is as strong as a horse, and deems himself descended from Caligula's ennobled steed ? Or Ephikhodof, that marvellous grotesque ? Or Yasha,

78

that child of the steppes with the mentality of a Parisian *gigolo ?* Or Firs, who is your " old retainer " with a difference ? Madame Ranevsky, that indolent reed, leads the women easily, though Barbara is a great pool of melancholy, and Anya is vaguely foredoomed to unhappiness. Even Charlotte the governess, whiling away her antiquated virginity with card-tricks and ventriloquism, is a terrifying figure. Yet how real they are ! Mad, indeed, should we be to deny that but for the grace of God. . . .

Well, here these creatures are fixed in this play more enduringly than if they had walked the earth in flesh and blood. They wander in and out, missing trains, hunting for mislaid goloshes, rhapsodising, soliloquising, telling one another that they are grown ugly or have taken to smelling like chickens, consenting to ruin, yet in all their ineffectiveness as sensible to sight and hearing, as much *there* as if they had put in an English morning's work and snatched the afternoon to return an effective card for the golf club's monthly medal.

But is not one in this play up against the old difficulty of trying to put into terms of logic a beauty which pours itself into one's being through every avenue of sense ? I want the reader to be chilled by that early-morning light stealing into the room still called the nursery, and to sadden with the glow of that melancholy sunset filtering through the shutters at the end. I want him to see that arabesque of trees against the moon, to hear Ephikhodof moan of requited love to the guitar which he miscalls a mandoline. I want him to rub his cheek against Trophimof's thin beard, to feel with his hands the woolly texture of the smock which Pishtchik wears beneath his frock-coat. Even if all this were achieved I should despair of getting the reader ro realise, away from the actual theatre, the delicate beauty of that scene in which these spirits in bondage dance home and orchard away to the tune of an old Viennese waltz. The fiddles die down, the partners separate and stand watching the governess at her imbecile card-tricks like the courtiers of Watteau fading beneath the trees which shall outlive them. But there, it's no use talking. *The Cherry Orchard* is an imperishable masterpiece, which will remain as long as men have eyes to see, ears to hear, and the will to comprehend beauty.

But let it not be supposed that the spectator will pass a doleful evening. He won't. These creatures have their comic side, which Tchehov is as quick to see as anybody. Four months before the first production of the play the author wrote to Madame Stanislavsky whose husband was to play Lopahkin : " It has turned out, not a drama but a comedy, in parts a farce." Those, then, who like laughing at a play, as I do, can laugh their heartiest at these often absurd people without fear of doing the low-brow thing. Ephikhodof, that bundle of misery, excellently played by Mr. James Whale, might have walked into this piece straight out of English musical comedy. The fellow cannot enter a room without tripping, hand a bouquet without dropping it, or play billiards without breaking his cue. Poor Alfred Lester played him often. He is only a small character, yet he has his place, and when he speaks the world centres round him for the space of that utterance. Each character shimmers with continuous life, and joins the others to form a kaleidoscope of which each speaker in turn is the centre.

The piece calls for the finest playing, and Mr. Fagan's company were often very fine. Miss Mary Grey, though physically too magnificent, subdued her soul to the required degree of slightness, and her pose in the second act and dumb grief in the third were lovely. The two daughters of Miss Virginia Isham and Miss Gwendolen Evans could not have been bettered. I am just a little bothered about the Gayef of Mr. Alan Napier and the Lopahkin of Mr. Fred O'Donovan. Was Gayef a trifle too seedy for a remnant of the old nobility? Was Lopahkin a wee bit too brutal? Mr. O'Donovan gave him a red-handed, destructive shade, whereas I suggest that he, too, belongs to the old order and will pass away with it. His cry of " Strike up, music ! " is ironical, not triumphant. He is ashamed of his success and would drown it. Perhaps the actor, trailed, *malgré lui*, and because of old association, too many clouds of Abbey Theatre boorishness. But within their own conceptions, which is what really matters, both Mr. Napier and Mr. O'Donovan acted very well indeed. Mr. John Gielgud's Perpetual Student was perfection itself, Mr. Smith's Pishtchik was immensely jolly, and Mr. Clarence's Firs must have drawn tears from the policeman in the gallery. In a repertory company one part must go astray, and Miss Ellis as the governess was miscast. She should have been elderly and ridiculous. But the performance as a whole gave immense delight, and the staging and lighting were admirable.

I am always being asked which is the best play in London. This is. For the high-brow? Yes, and for butcher, baker, and candlestick-maker as well. I suggest that *The Cherry Orchard* is one of the great plays of the world. Let your British stalwart consider the educated Chinaman who should have left his almond-trees to inquire into European culture. Shall we show him these listless Russian folk, or is it that Mr. Coward's exuberated ladies do our civilisation greater credit?

*May 25.*

# " The Sea-Gull "

## A PLAY BY ANTON TCHEHOV

### LITTLE THEATRE

TCHEHOV is to many people like a red rag to a bull. The performance of *The Sea-Gull* at the Little Theatre, on Monday last, drove a brother critic into a state of paranoia, in which he could see no difference between plays of this Russian dramatist and those of Dumas and Sardou. Yet one would affirm that Tchehov is like Tchehov and nobody else, and that the reason he gives extraordinary pleasure is because he is exactly true to life. But that will not do for an all-sufficing description of this or any other dramatist, unless we are prepared to accept the proposition that all dramatists who are like life are like one another. Which would be absurd.

What then is Tchehov's peculiar merit ? Calderon tells us that this playwright is " centrifugal instead of self-centred " ; Mr. Dukes explains that as Andriev is the symbolist of the spiritual crisis, so Tchehov is its realist : Mr. William Archer was apparently so exhausted by his exhaustive study of *The Old Drama and the New* that he forbore to tackle the Russian giant

83

and left him out altogether. Probably it is this writer's inaction which is his *forte* and at the same time the red flag which so affrights our British bull. Ordinary people leading bustling lives appear to go to the theatre to see somebody " get a move on." Some critics have preferred *The Sea-Gull* above the rest of Tchehov's plays for the reason that it has a plot. I find myself in different case, and hold that *The Sea-Gull* is less enchanting than some other Tchehov dramas because of its, dare I say, irrelevant excursion into outward happenings. Inward life is this dramatist's true domain.

The " note " of this play is given in the opening exchanges. Masha and Medvedenko are returning from a walk. He says to her, " Why do you always wear black ? " and she replies, " I am in mourning for my life. I am unhappy." This is the key to everything in this play. All the characters but two have fought a losing battle against life, and are in mourning for their defeat. What a crew they are, both the successful and unsuccessful ! Madam Arkadin, the egotistical, shallow actress jealous of her son's pretentions to genius ; the son who has the soul of an artist and no ability ; Trigorin, that essentially successful and second-rate writer without soul or conscience ; Nina, that young woman stage-struck like one living in Balham or Kensington ; Sorin, a weak-minded voluptuary who would make up in old age for the cowardices of a well-spent youth ; Masha, the steward's daughter moping after Konstantin ; Dorn, the one-time handsome young doctor, now a philosopher of insufferable tedium ; Medvedenko, or poverty's withered limb. Yes, they are indeed a job lot, but as they sit about the stage lolling and smoking, and each one babbling of his private concerns with nobody listening to anybody else, one knows oneself to be in the presence of people who are really alive.

Take the beginning of the second act where they are all sitting in the garden in the heat of midday. Dorn is pretending to read and is continually interrupted by the others, each of whom speaks his thoughts aloud. Masha is of opinion that she drags her life after her like a dead weight, or the train of an endless dress. Madam Arkadin explains to everybody that the secret of remaining well preserved is never to allow oneself to become dowdy. Nobody is interested. Sorin snores in a wheel-chair. Masha complains that her leg has gone to sleep. The others yawn. They can stand the tedium no longer and order horses to go into the town. But the horses are carrying rye and the steward cannot spare them. A ridiculous squall of nerves arises. And so on and so forth. I can only say that watching these people I am a-tingle with excitement, each character telling me as much about himself as Hamlet, and with the expenditure of one-tenth of Hamlet's words. Yet I find a respected colleague writing that " this is a stuffed play. There is no blood, no light, no truth in it." Well, it is true to me, and I suppose Signor Pirandello would say that that is the limit of lawful pronouncement.

I, at any rate, hardly know a more moving situation than that in which Konstantin is compelled to tell Dorn, inquiring idly, what has happened to the Nina whom Konstantin loves. Almost equally moving is the scene in which Konstantin and Nina rehearse together the opening lines of the boy's play in which the girl acted years ago on that summer evening by the lake. Disaster has come upon her, and upon him is the full sense of failure ; yet for a moment they touch something for which there is no name—a recollection of early happiness. " Tchehov," says my colleague, " as a dramatist was a faker, and it is high time someone called his bluff. This *Sea-Gull* is for the gullible." Yet I should have thought the opening lines of this play within a play were sufficient in themselves to warn us of the presence of genius. Let me quote them :—

> Men and lions, eagles and partridges, antlered deer, geese, spiders, the silent fishes dwelling in the water, starfish, and tiny creatures invisible to the eye—these and every form of life, ay, every form of life, have ended their melancholy round and become extinct. . . . Thousands of centuries have passed since this earth bore any living being on its bosom. All in vain does yon pale moon light her lamp. No longer do the cranes wake and cry in the meadows ; the hum of the may-beetle is silent in the linden groves.

Stage craft ? The play bristles with it. Take Medvedenko's unexpected question, " What salary does a choirman get ? " This single remark illuminates the whole of the wretched fellow's poverty. It is like a stone dropped into a well, but the well is one of perfect meaning. To those who deny the existence of these futile Russians, or, accepting their existence, deny that its contemplation gives them pleasure, one cannot give any satisfactory answer. To me this play is like an October walk through dripping beech woods. *De gustibus*, you might say, and all the rest of it. Let not the symbolism of the sea-gull affright timid folk too greatly. It is simple enough, and, alternately, if you find it too difficult you can ignore it. At least it is not, as Calderon points out, ugly and half-insane, like Ibsen's symbolism of the Tower, from the top of which an elderly architect falls whilst his sweetheart down below hops and skips about and waves a little flag.

High-brows inform me that they have seen better performances of this play at Hong Kong and Nijninovgorod. But I, unfamiliar with these watering-places, must content me with what I see. Miss Miriam Lewes brought to the part of the actress all her grace of movement and diction, if possibly a trifle too much sincerity. Madam Arkadin might, one thought, have been shallower. Mr. John Gielgud played the ineffective son with great sensitiveness and beautifully controlled emotion. Miss Valérie Taylor, as Nina, gave a performance which, if the piece had only been rubbish, would now bring her at a bound into the ranks of our foremost actresses. But as she is hampered by playing in a piece recognised all over Europe as a work of genius,

I am afraid this young lady will just have to take her chance. Deft and comprehending performances were given by Miss Margaret Swallow and Mr. James Whale. Perhaps Trigorin was not very good, but there, one cannot have everything.

*October* 19.

# " The Godless "

## A Play by MADAME KAREN BRAMSON

### Wyndham's Theatre

HERE is an old-fashioned play ! One would put the spiritual date of *The Godless* at 1882, the year in which Edna Lyall wrote *Donovan*. The hero of this three-volume tract was a young gentleman who, before he was five years old, would wake his nurse in the middle of the night by proclaiming in excited tones that if sheep were thirty-nine shillings each it would take £87 15*s.* to buy forty-five of them. The child then turned his mighty intellect upon the constitution of the universe, which he decided was an entirely material affair, persisting in this way of thinking until his worst enemy fell a victim to the small-pox. This convinced Donovan of the error of his metaphysic, and on the last page he took his sweetheart in his arms, saying : " Are you ready, darling, to be the wife of a radical, to be looked down on perhaps as the wife of a sometime atheist ? " In the early 'eighties this book was considered exceedingly " advanced," and children who were in the process of being nicely brought up were not allowed to look into it. The interdiction was right, though the reason for it was wrong. Religious speculation like Miss Lyall's must always be bad for the child-mind, not because it is too modern, but because it is too muddled.

The quality of Mme. Bramson's thinking in the play called *The Godless*, produced on Tuesday afternoon, does not improve upon those earlier cerebrations. Here also is a little boy who takes to philosophy from his tenderest years. But meningitis supervenes, so that it is his father who, in Bacon's phrase, cogitateth and considereth, while his mother, employing the faculty of her fancy, also cogitateth. The father is an old hand at the game, having gone through it all before on the death of his first wife. One by one he trots out all the arguments which have served the turn of so many schoolboy and other immature debaters. How reconcile Nature, red in tooth and claw, with the doctrine of all-pervading Love ? How reconcile care for the individual with war, pestilence, and famine ? The father is logical in so far as he goes, but he does not seem to realise that he is not the first to have banged this door or to be aware of the expedients which Man has invented to keep it open—faint trust in the larger hope and all the rest of it. And then he went beyond agnosticism, which we can all respect, into the presumptuousness of atheism, which sooner or later always finds its reward. " *Si Dieu n'existait pas il fallait l'inventer !* " said the ironic Frenchman, and it is not in irony but in agony that the unbeliever cries to his newly-made God. But one takes it that there is an admirable quality of human feeling and a poor quality of human thinking in the position of a father who will decide a matter entirely beyond human competence according to whether his child does or does not recover from an illness.

The woman's side of the matter is not conditioned by reason at all. She nags at her husband for not having prayed for the recovery of his first wife with such persistence as to suggest that the poor lady's passing has done her, the second wife, a disservice. Her husband being too old for her she has frankly taken a lover with whom she would go away were it not for the child whom she will not surrender to its father's atheistic influence. She is of opinion, and takes no pains to conceal it, that the child's meningitis is a visitation upon the father's incredulity, and so on and so forth. Whereby the part ultimately flounders in a morass of sentiment, hysterics, and bad logic. The father could, of course, have brought the play to an end at any moment by asking : " Surely, if anybody is to be punished for my unbelief it should be I ? Why, then, haven't I got meningitis ? " Instead of which one finds him preparing for a conversion upon lines which take away from him even that trifle of intellectual respect which he had.

The play is of a devastating dullness and, as the reader must have guessed, is also open to one really grave objection. This is the introduction of the afflicted boy. That a child whom we have seen in health should become an idiot and din its little moanings into our ears is a thing so pitiful as to exceed dramatic propriety. The incident is intended to illustrate parental cogitabundity ; what it actually does is to swamp any such consideration. It becomes less than nothing to the spectator whether the parents of such a victim are free-thinkers or fire-worshippers, cannibals or Thugs. It is not permissible to harrow the senses with the spectacle of a deformed infant so that (*a*) the husband may argue that if the wife had not been distracted by her lover the child would not have fallen out of the perambulator, and (*b*) the wife may retort that if he had given his Saturday afternoons to her instead of to golf there would have been no lover and no accident. It has been accepted from Aristotle downwards that tragedy shall present a moral issue, and is not concerned with unrelated phenomena of suffering. Schiller tells us that in the same ratio that the senses are visibly roused, so the influence of morality will be proportionately diminished. In other words, the more our sense of pity was moved by the guiltless suffering of the child, the less was our interest in the moral speculations bandied about its head. The spectacle of a father clasping an idiot son to his bosom and proposing to order his religious belief according as he does or does not recover, awakens displeasure at an attitude which is both callous and irreverent. Who, in the presence of this afflicted brain, can have any thought to spare for what the father may think of Paley's Evidences ?

The piece, which was always half-dead, was not too well treated by the actors. Mr. Lion, trying to put some sort of life into it, failed to get the one quality which would have made the scientist probable—the kind of granite scepticism which Mr. Norman McKinnel does so well.    Miss Frances Doble acted very cleverly, and must not be blamed because each sentence made one dislike the character more than the one before.    Mr. J. Fisher White gave his theologically-minded and sententious physician a manner which would have been entirely suited to the bedside of a dying Archbishop, and Mr. J. H. Roberts did well to retain his self-possession when confronted with an astronomer whose mind was apparently constructed out of Berlin wool.

*December* 15.

# " L'École des Cocottes "

## A Play. Adapted by H. M. HARWOOD
### From the French of MM. Armont and Gerbidon

BRITISH burgess-hood was present in full
strength on Sunday evening last to witness a
play which the Censor had refused to license for reasons
sufficient doubtless unto the mind of authority, but at
which it was wildly impossible to make even the faintest
guess.   Only the other day Mr. George Morrison was
reminding us that there was a time when *La Dame aux
Camélias* was not allowed to be performed in English
in this country, though no objection was raised to the
operatic version of the same story.   " *Ce qui est trop
bête pour être dit, on le chante,*" said Beaumarchais, and
the English appear to have gone one better by deciding
that whatever is too immoral to be said may be sung.
But even English prunes and prisms cannot withstand
ridicule for ever, and the late George du Maurier completely discomfited Mrs. Grundy when he showed Mrs.
Gorgius Midas entering the theatre, refusing the book
of words of this piece, and saying haughtily : " We
have come to see the acting ;  we do not wish to understand the play."   However, the piece was ultimately
performed, opinion being revised so far as to recognise

that consumption, like charity, covers a multitude of sins.

After Marguerite came Paula Tanqueray, who, we remember, had in turn been Paula Dartry, Paula Ethurst, Paula Ardale, and Paula Jarman. The lady had not been married to any of her gentlemen friends, but the Censor licensed the play, possibly because of the pistol-shot at the end. There is no pistol-shot at the end of *L'École des Cocottes*, but there is a piece of untruth which is almost as shocking. A young woman is shown rising upon the stepping-stones of discarded lovers to states of increasing dreariness and boredom, and the process is crystallised in a smug little line about leaving happiness to the unsuccessful. Isn't it time we dropped the pretence that Nell Gwyn would have been happier if she had stuck to her orange-basket, Emma Hamilton to her dusting, and the Du Barry to her dressmaking? In musical comedy it would appear that this pretence does not obtain, so that our young people must pierce each for himself to the barren disillusion and aching melancholy which, it is moral to suppose, underlie the pearls and the refrain in three-four time. Let us improve upon the old dictum so that it runs: Whatever in England is too naughty to be acted on the stage proper is the proper stuff for musical comedy.

Those who may be disappointed at not having seen this bright and entertaining if rather old-fashioned French piece can get an admirable idea of what it was like by reading Halévy's little story, *Madame Cardinal*, in the volume entitled *Madame et Monsieur Cardinal*.

This collection of sketches of French life was published in 1872, and by the year 1900 had gone into fifty-nine editions. Virginie Cardinal is a dancer at the opera, and the story is the account of her successive love affairs with one Crochard, a deplorable actor, whose highest achievement is a guest in *Lucrecia Borgia*, with one Monsieur Paul, who is by way of being a gentleman, and, finally, with the Marquis Cavalcanti. The story is extraordinarily witty and amusing and " as good as a play." Ginette in the piece on Sunday makes the same kind of painful ascent. But whereas Halévy got all his fun out of the reflections of Monsieur and Madame Cardinal anent the progress of their daughter, MM. Armont and Gerbidon are content with the thinner humours which accompany the process of making a lady out of a shopgirl. One would say that the Halévy story is entirely true throughout and that not a word of it rings false, whereas the modern play is true in everything except its moral implication at the end.

Miss Gladys Cooper did all that could be done with the part of Ginette. She looked very charming and natural in the first act, in which she lived up to the ever-distressing chink of those silly glass bangles. In the second act she very cleverly assumed the air of vulgar magnificence proper to this stage of Ginette's development. And in the third act this always-improving actress arrived finally at that grand manner which is only within the reach of those who start from small beginnings. Here Miss Cooper looked more than usually beautiful. Her playing was sensitive and intelligent throughout the whole evening, and possibly the only suggestions of incompleteness lay in the fact that she did not at any time alter the intonations of her voice, and would always pronounce " Amélie " to rhyme with " family," and " Rue " as though it were the little herb of grace.  Mr. Leslie Faber, whom I suspect to have been nearer Paris than Boulogne, contributed a character-study which might have come straight out of Halévy, than which I can think of no higher praise.  Messrs. Aubrey Mather and Athole Stewart acted very well indeed, but Mr. John Gielgud was too noble for the type of Paris *gigolo* who keeps a mistress on three hundred francs a month.  Miss Dorothy Hamilton gave an extremely clever performance of a girl whom Nature had obviously ordained for the paths of virtue.  To my way of thinking this was easily the best and truest character in the piece. To commiserate with the inability to transgress is not the English temper, and it may well have been this character which frightened the Censor.  Yet one has known thousands of Ugly Sisters in musical comedy, to jeer at whom has always been considered proper and legitimate.  The whole play, with the exception of the bit of sentimental fudge at the end, seemed to me to be as near truth as makes no matter.  To refuse to license this piece in the face of some other recent comedies, less true and more demoralising, to which no objection has been taken is almost the silliest thing I have ever heard of, even in the world of the theatre.

*December 13.*

97

# "The Verge"

## A Play by SUSAN GLASPELL

### The Pioneer Players

YEARS ago I remember sending a postcard to an obstinate controversialist : " Goethe said that he was not such a fool that he could not change his opinions." My friend retorted, also by postcard : " My opinions are not so foolish that they need to be changed." I am to confess that, in view of certain modest trumpetings last summer, I went to the performance of Susan Glaspell's play with something approaching trepidation. As it turned out, trepidation was unnecessary. I stand my ground. *The Verge* is a great play.

Not a limpid, impeccable, easily understandable masterpiece, but then I never declared that it was. Is it "unwholesome"? Possibly, but then if plays like *The Sea Urchin* are "wholesome" the contrary charge does not worry me. Let it be admitted that the heroine of the piece is for most of the time on the edge of madness and that at the end she tumbles over. What of that? Or again, that she is like a Johnny Head-in-Air who does not know where his feet are going.

What, again, of that? The whole point about this piece is that it does at least traffic with the clouds, whereas your normal " wholesome " play either leaves ideas out of account or exhibits the human mind grovelling in the mud. Admitted that *The Verge* is wrapped up in a kind of lambent obscurity. Admitted that Claire is a visionary whose visions, if fulfilled, would end in equal annihilation of good and bad, in reduction of the universe to a nothingness from which even the absurd is excluded. Some of my colleagues have made these and other equally damning, and equally easy, charges against this play, one of the most esteemed of them going so far as to imply that the whole work is unmitigated bosh. This I will not admit, mitigated bosh being the utmost concession. The essential criticism, the difficult, anxious job, I venture to submit, is to point out the mitigations.

*The Verge* is the work of a fine and sensitive mind, preoccupied with fine and sensitive things. The insanity which throttles Edgeworthy is of the same order as that which makes Hilda Wangel send Solness to his death on the tower. Solness, you remember, has declared that building homes for human beings is not worth a rap, and then comes the moan, " Nothing really built ; *nor anything sacrificed for the chance of building.*" Those last words are the key to Susan Glaspell's play. Solness went on to build castles in the air, and sacrificed his life in the attempt. Claire holds that to go on titivating a world for present humanity to live in is not worth a rap, and she dreams of a fresh race which shall have reminiscence of the most fragrant of humanity, but no more. It is to this ideal that she sacrifices her lover. He is an image of Beauty which gets in the way of Beauty. He who should be a gate stops the place. . . .

Now, on jury-level, what is Claire but an egomaniacal murderess ? But what was Hilda, who bade a harmless old gentleman, and her host moreover, climb to the top of the tower, knowing well that he would fall and be killed ? The point is whether you would rather go mad for three hours with Ibsen and Susan Glaspell or remain sane with the author of *The Sea Urchin*. *Of course* the play has crudenesses and violences as well as surpassing beauties. Nobody whose genius was less than Ibsen's could have hoped to tackle this theme at all ; and the essentially critical thing, I repeat, is to compute the play's virtues from the ground up rather than calculate by how much they decline from the top of achievement. The American writer made her case more difficult by applying it to the whole human race, whereas the Norwegian confined it to the individual. It is the difference between the small shop and the big stores. In this instance the shop is kept by a man of prodigious genius and the stores are run by a not yet fully matured writer of great talent. But both deal in the same kind of groceries. And, personally, I like upon occasion to have to do with minds so predisposed, and leave the " common crofts, the vulgar thorpes " for that appropriate country where man's thought

Rarer, intenser,
Self-gathered for an outbreak, as it ought,
Chafes in the censer.

The performance is to be repeated at the Regent Theatre on Monday evening and Tuesday afternoon, and intending visitors might do worse than refresh their recollection of Browning's *Grammarian's Funeral*. They will then be most fully equipped to appreciate the full measure of Miss Sybil Thorndike's superb performance in the part of one who

> . . . ventured neck or nothing—heaven's success
> Found, or earth's failure.

And, in conclusion, I reaffirm my original statement. This is a great play. It has the improbable for its plane, but that in this instance is a plateau of which the accidents are steeples of thought, not pits of fatuity.

*March* 29.

# Modern Plays

# " Tess of the d'Urber-villes "

## A Tragedy by THOMAS HARDY

### Barnes Theatre

*TESS of the d'Urbervilles* was a great venture. I am a poor hand at literary criticism, and offer the following observation without any great belief in its value. But this thought was very insistently with me at Barnes—that though the date of *Tess* in its complete form is the very early 'nineties, the work is utterly removed from the spirit which we now recognise as " ninety-ish." The note of those days was struck unhappily by the flowers of æstheticism, always sickly and now for ever perished. Did we know their transience then, and were we conscious beneath the surface of those giant roots thrown out by the masters of the new literature which was to come crowding upon the heels of Dickens, Thackeray, and George Eliot ? Is it wrong to see in Mr. Hardy the first realist to cast the sombre mantle over these facts of life which the Victorians saw sentimentally, and the preceding age had viewed with gusto ? Times change, and it is possible that Mr. Hardy's great book dates. The novelist found tragedy in a situation which could not be tragic to-day, for the reason that the situation would not be there, the mentality of Angel Clare being definitely of a past age. But if the book may be said to date, at least it dates nobly. It was the production of a lofty mind, and as such it is immune from the assault of Time. Tragedy, once great, can suffer no decrease.

*Tess* is no village drama, though one takes Marlott, the home of the Durbeyfields, to be no more than a hamlet. Everything in the book is on a big scale, the scope of human passion matching the sweep of the Wessex plain. Tess herself is a rich creature of the soil, a peony in the chaplet of village beauty. Everything about her is big—her capacity for love, anguish, sacrifice, even hate. Remember how little she says when Angel comes back to find her Alec d'Urberville's mistress. " Too late, too late ! " she drones, then a few words which are the scaffold rather than the body of an explanation, and last her single sentence : " He has won me back to him." This, of course, is the classic standby of every play of misunderstanding. It is the whole meretricious burden of Armand Duval's case against Marguerite. But under the hand of a great writer the worn phrase is shaped anew, and we feel that with its utterance the last punishment for no sin has been visited upon the innocent. When Dumas used the phrase we knew it for a pretty and an effective trick ; when Mr. Hardy uses it we feel that Tess is, as the great French actress Clarion said of a Greek heroine, the victim of a pitiless goddess. That the English writer did not reject the pagan conception is shown by his choice of Stonehenge for the final scene of his tragedy and by the pregnant sentence at the close " ' Justice ' was done, and the President of the Immortals (in Æschylean phrase) had ended his sport with Tess."

How to get this great book upon the stage was indeed a problem. Mr. Hardy, acting as his own adapter, chose the literal way, crowding his four acts with the story's incident and not even omitting the country dancing. Yet even so those two scenes which one remembers most achingly had to be omitted—Tess's agony at the threshing of the wheat-rack under her former lover's eyes and the hacking in the swede-field. Probably the young people who may not have known the book still found this stage play lacerating enough, though Angel's attitude can hardly be within their comprehension. But to the rest of us this all seemed strangely diminished. Certainly the only way to complete success lay in Tess herself. One insists again that she is a great creature, since Æschylean gods cannot be held to visit their sport upon weaklings. The ardours of summer passion and the rigours of bleak days in wind-swept fields should be implicit in the bodily presence of this woman ; more can be conveyed to us by what she *is* than by what she must say or do. One actress, long unfamiliar to our stage—I mean Miss Mona Limerick —could have looked and played the part ideally. So, too, could Mrs. Patrick Campbell before her art took drawing-room ways. And to-day perhaps only Miss Sybil Thorndike has the technical resource and sweep of emotion which are needed to deal with that great third act. Miss Ffrangçon-Davies, though her intellectual mastery of the part was never to seek, had insufficient physical presence, and her acting lacked wealth of accomplishment. This Tess was little almost to insignificance, her deepest note being that of the petulant. But I seem to remember that Mr. Hardy calls Liza-Lu a slighter and spiritualised version of her sister, which in the case of this Tess would be impossible. It has often been noted that effects which are good in the novel are poor on the stage. Mr. Hardy tells us of a pouted, deep-red mouth, and the way the lower lip had of thrusting the middle of the top one upward. Curiously enough, Miss Ffrangçon-Davies has always had this little trick which, on the stage, has the effect of reducing woe to peevishness. It should be understood that the actress did nothing wrong, and achieved many perfect things in a little scale.

If I read Angel Clare aright, he should have great charm, overlaid by an inheritance of moral convention. Mr. Ion Swinley gave us the convention without the charm, and I suggest that he would have been better cast as d'Urberville. This personage was grotesqued rather than impersonated by Mr. Austin Trevor, who made the fellow look like the Badminton picture of Mr. Macfie about to putt, and was melodramatic throughout. Mr. Stanley Lathbury and Miss Margaret Carter did very well as the Durbeyfields, but far and away the best performance was Mr. John Le Hay's Labourer. This was a great comic creation, and for the first time the house felt itself to be in the presence of fine acting. Miss Drusilla Wills and Miss Lizzie Webster also did excellently as two old crones, and perhaps it was in these three that Wessex came most to life. It is never fair to blame a producer unless one knows the amount of his freedom, but I cannot imagine that Mr. A. E. Filmer, left to himself, would not have cut out the entirely ineffective country dancing. It was a terrible blunder not to end the third act on the exit of Tess ; the landlady's discovery belongs to the novel, and in the theatre could be only anti-climax. Mr. Aubrey Hammond did as well as possible with an eighteen-foot stage, attaining perfect success with the Stonehenge scene, where three bits of cardboard gave all that was wanted.

*September 7.*

# "The Prisoners of War"

## A Play by J. R. ACKERLEY

### Three Hundred Club

*T*HE *Prisoners of War* is a piece of which one would not miss moment, incident, or personage. It is an arresting and dreadful story of the actions and reactions of a tiny group of men cut off from their kind and fenced in by the appalling solitude of Swiss mountains. Yes, the solitude at Murren must have been awful.

Or so Mr. Ackerley postulates. It could easily be objected to this piece that the material circumstances of the prisoners were such as to drive mad only those who, not being prisoners, had already reached the halfway house. What were the conditions of confinement? These officers lived in a pleasant hotel, played lawn tennis, bridge, and poker, went ski-ing, were invited to dances, had plenty to eat and drink, and enjoyed exactly the same time as that for which your winter tourist will pay large sums of money. Do sane men go mad out of boredom? Not often even in brick gaols, much less often on the tennis courts of Murren. Besides, must not ennui have been mitigated by the

thought that to hang about a pleasant countryside is less
dreadful than to hang upon a wire entanglement? Mr.
Ackerley's premise is one in which we cannot believe.
His conclusion it is which is authentic tragedy. It
jumps to the eyes that the problem is one not of depres-
sion but of repression.

Two out of the five officers, the Flying Man and the
Married Man, were as decent fellows as ever revoked
or foot-faulted. The Canadian gink—or whatever
he would have called himself—was a bit of a handful and
an offence to polite ears, but his kind has been put up
with before. The Cub was another matter. He
was a thorough-going little cad, impervious alike to
kindness and snubbing. But even so, tragedy would
not have ensued if the Captain had not been afflicted
by the least understood of abnormalities. Now it has
always seemed to me that the playgoer should accept
without quibble the hypothesis of his author and confine
debate to inference and conclusion. Thus: A. hates B.
and murders him. Our preoccupation must be with
what happens to A.'s mind after the murder; whether A.
justly hated B. is not to the point, that which is postulated on the rising of the curtain being a state of hate
between A. and B. intense to the degree of murder.
Surely it would be puerile to argue that repulsion
between A. and B. is a fit subject for tragedy, and attraction not. It is all a matter of handling. "Have you
heard the argument? Is there no offence in't?"
asks the King in *Hamlet*. The argument of *The
Prisoners of War* is conducted on the high and tragic

plane, and the mind, being touched to tragedy, finds no the offence provoked by the comedies *à la mode*.

Mr. George Hayes is one of the most interesting young actors on the English stage to-day. His performance in the part of the Captain was one for which not even his brilliant studies of Aaron in *Titus Andronicus* and of the mad doctor in the *Mental Athletes* had prepared us. I do not know that I should choose Mr. Hayes for Orlando or Ferdinand, but I feel that when the time comes for an actor to handle Strindberg and Pirandello, or to revive Ibsen, here is one who must not be overlooked. His performance was as subtle as it was discriminating, taking early flight into those regions where man suspends his smaller judgments and gives rein to larger pity. Not for a long time have I seen anything more wholly beautiful than that last act in which the wretched man, now beyond human companionship, sought communion with his plant. With delicate, mad hands, surely he had his posies, we could have said with Dowson. Not for a long time have I seen anything more wholly pathetic than Mr. Ivor Barnard's cameo of the married officer suddenly bereaved. Health, straightforward health, came into the play with the flying officer of Mr. Colin Keith-Johnson. This actor wears about him some of the healing power which Mr. Lewis Casson possesses so abundantly ; both players make you feel that no set of circumstances to which they lend the sanction of their presence can be wholly unbearable. Acting such as this has something of the quality of the sheet anchor ;

the mind, though voyaging in perilous seas, may come to safety at will. Very considerable praise should be given to Mr. Robert Harris, who in his portrait of the disagreeable young man closed every avenue of ingratiation, and achieved a success of pure art.

There were only two women in the piece—an adventuress and a dowdy, matronly body from some vaguely beneficent association. These were played with extraordinary sympathy and realism by Miss Leah Bateman and Miss Marie Ault. The name of the producer, Mr. Frank Birch, is new to me. Doubtless this is my fault, and I hasten to say that I desire better acquaintance. It is impossible to imagine that the play could have been better produced, or better acted.

*July* 5.

# "Juno and the Paycock"

## A TRAGEDY BY SEAN O'CASEY

### ROYALTY THEATRE

THREE-QUARTERS of a century ago Henry
Morley, in his *Journal of a London Playgoer*,
made the discovery that the English temper jibs at un-
diluted tragedy. Whether for good or ill, the English
audience, says Morley, has a habit of looking out for
something upon which to feed its appetite for the
absurd. The orthodox writer of melodrama satisfies
that hunger with a comic underplot, and by so doing
" saves his terrors whole." It is impossible, I suggest,
to imagine an Englishman taking his wife and family
to a State theatre on a Sunday afternoon to follow the
humourless progress of *Polyeucte* and *Heraclius*,
*Bajazet* and *Mithridate*. We are not built that way,
and Shakespeare knew it when he gave Lear his Fool
and wrote in the porter's scene in *Macbeth*. Morley
ends an admirable argument with a sentence which is
highly significant to-day : " There must be a deeper
earnestness than plays can demand, in whatever serious
thing Englishmen are to look at without exercise of that
sense of the humorous which is part of their life ; so

natural a part that every man in every grade of society is regarded as a bore who lacks it ; and the very phrase with thousands even among our educated men for not finding a thing acceptable is ' seeing no fun ' in it." In other words, while musical comedy is all the rage, musical tragedy is inconceivable.

The Irish, who are popularly supposed not to know what they want on their side of the Channel, would appear to have a very accurate idea of what we English want on ours. Or, at least one of them, Mr. Sean O'Casey, has an adequate notion. " Juno and the Paycock " is as much a tragedy as Macbeth, but it is a tragedy taking place in the porter's family. Mr. O'Casey's extraordinary knowledge of English taste— that he wrote his play for the Abbey Theatre, Dublin, is not going to be allowed to disturb my argument—is shown by the fact that the tragic element in it occupies at the most some twenty minutes, and that for the remaining two hours and a half the piece is given up to gorgeous and incredible fooling. " Juno," it should perhaps be explained here, is a woman of the Dublin slums, born, courted and married in the month of June ; her husband is called " the Paycock " because he prefers taking the floor of a public-house in strutting magnificence to doing a day's work. The tragedy that befalls their son and daughter is felt in repercussion by the mother, and not at all by the father. The daughter's affair is comparatively commonplace. She is courted by the lawyer's clerk who brings the news of the family's sudden prosperity, and is at once abandoned by him when that prosperity proves chimerical.

The son's tragedy is conditioned by the drama's place and time. The scene is a tenement house in Dublin, and the time is 1922, during the fighting between the Free Staters and the Republican Die-hards. One is a little uncertain about the value and amount of the tragic surprise in this play. I happened to have read the piece, and therefore knew the fate in store for Johnny Boyle—which is to be dragged out and shot for treachery—and the full value to be assigned to his terrors. It would be interesting to know at what point exactly a spectator coming fresh to the play would connect Johnny's state of panic with the shooting of the boy lying dead in the same tenement. Would such a spectator get an inkling of the connection before the entrance of the Irregular Mobiliser at the end of the second act ? To any one who is aware of what is to come the comforting of the terrified boy by his mother in the middle of this act has an extraordinary poignancy, lacking, I suggest, if the cause of the boy's terror is not revealed. But perhaps the shadow is sufficiently forecast ; I simply cannot tell. Probably, Mr. O'Casey knows from performances in Dublin how far his intentions here are fulfilled. My own feeling is that as the value of surprise is very small in comparison with the value of apprehension, the tragic matter should be exposed to the audience from the beginning. There are some tremendous moments in this piece, and the ironic close—in which the drunken porter returns to his lodging unconscious of his son's death, daughter's flight to river or streets, and wife's desertion—is the work of a master.

Mr. Arthur Sinclair has never before been seen in such a fine part. He stands four-square to all the winds of the grotesque, ruminating in a bemused rapture of self-delight. He has the hooded eye of some intoxicated owl wise in its own conceit. This, we feel, is a full man, though that wherewith he is filled be folly. Miss Sara Allgood lags but little behind in the way of humour ; her geniality has its bite of shrewdness while her causticities hardly sear. I do not find myself quite in agreement with Miss Allgood's rendering of the distressful side of her part. Here Juno seemed to me to abandon the character and accent of a Dublin charwoman and to make ascent to Duse-like ineffabilities of grief. It is in my mind that at the news of her son's murder such a woman would be inclined to " carry on " in the pre-war sense, and give sorrow noisy and vulgar words. The fault is probably Mr. O'Casey's, since he has given Miss Allgood nothing to be noisy and vulgar with. Instead, he makes Mrs. Boyle repeat what that other bereaved mother had said in an earlier act. Sentiment and words are in themselves sublime, and may easily be supposed to rise in the mind of one whose grief, like Mrs. Tancred's, is some hours old. But it is difficult to believe that any newly-stricken mother would at once fall to praying for murdering hate to be taken away, though the echo has a certain dramatic value. Miss Allgood's performance, granted feasibility, was very fine

There were many admirable pieces of acting in the play, but I must be content to single out two—an amusing character-creation by Mr. Sydney Morgan and a piece of careful truth by Mr. Harry Hutchinson. *Bis dat qui cito dat*, says the Latin proverb, which, being translated, means that from the managerial point of view that playgoer visits the theatre twice who visits it quickly. Messrs. J. B. Fagan and Dennis Eadie, who present this piece, are entitled to the fullest measure of support. For this is a great play, in which both educated and uneducated will see any amount of that fun which Morley declared to be our heritage.

*November* 16.

# " The Round Table "

## A Play by LENNOX ROBINSON

### Wyndham's Theatre

HERE is a technically imperfect play which is many miles, streets, oceans—or whatever unit of comparison you prefer—better than 99 per cent. of West End successes. Yet this piece—all shame to playgoers—is not doing roaring business. Why? Because, presumably, it does not deal with life as it is lived in gilded cages by vulgar little singing-birds. Because the life with which it has the temerity to deal is the middle-class life known to thousands of families in these islands. Because it keys up that life to a nice pitch of comedy and exaggeration. Because half the characters are first-class comic creations, and the other half, being familiar, amuse without fatiguing. Because the dialogue is uniformly witty. Because the whole piece is *exceedingly good fun*. Because for about ten minutes we are asked to use about one hundredth part of our brains. The last, of course, is the snag. No audience has ever cared tuppence about technical imperfections.

119

An alternative title for this piece might be Miss Jesse's *Anyhouse*, principally because Russian anarchists *don't* break in to bomb a purse-proud family and destroy a victimised servant-maid. Or Mr. Robinson could have called it *At Mrs. Drennan's*, since chiefly talk occurs. How well we know the Drennans ! The old lady, of course, is Mrs. Nickleby all over again. Her talk runs on, not so much like a stream, which has direction, as the aimless waste flooding a meadow. Mrs. Drennan cannot undo the parcel of her mind without giving you the whole contents. Could anything be better than that account of Mr. Drennan's continued faith in himself ? As his relict goes over the tale of successive failures, incidentally getting that tritest of Browning quotations all wrong, we behold a second Micawber marching breastforward from one bankruptcy to another, never doubting clouds will gather, rising only to fall. Even after fourteen years tears of pride still gather in his widow's eyes.

Then there is Miss Williams-Williams, or " Billy-Billy," the most helpless of poor relations, whose very *raison d'être* lies in being penniless and forlorn. She, indeed, is " a piece of impertinent correspondency," not belonging to the Drennan family by any of the recognisable ties, yet part and parcel of it now and for ever. Don't tell me the character is farcical. No family is so unhappy as not to possess a " Billy-Billy," for she is at heart a dear. Then there is De Courcy Drennan—what genius lies in that " De Courcy " !—a lump of unalloyed selfishness ; and Bee

Drennan, that monument to slatternliness ; and Jonty Drennan, that Pinchbeck idealist weltering in physical culture, esoterics, and Stravinsky. Covent Garden gallery on German nights knows well his kind.

The play is concerned with the frantic efforts of this helpless family to prevent Daisy, the one sound member, from deserting it to get married. It is Daisy who makes us use our brains. There are moments when she gets glimpses of the immorality of self-sacrifice, and she realises that the family to which she is attached is really a prison. And there appears on the other side of the window-pane a figure who is the embodiment of all that Daisy might have been but for the family, and, but for the family, *might yet be !* The woman has no existence ; she is a visualisation of Daisy's " other self," a false creation proceeding, as Macbeth says, from the heat-oppressed brain, from, in to-day's words, the state of enervation produced by dancing over-long attendance on her helpless brood. She has one passage of avowed beauty descriptive of a life of freedom, but the passage lasts only three minutes or so, and should not be an insuperable bugbear. I know perfectly well what I shall be told. I shall be told that Mr. Robinson has attempted to make an amalgam out of two compounds each of which, though good in itself, can never have anything to do with the other. That, to a certain extent, is true. But my point is that it is better to dine off alternate slices of perfectly good onion and perfectly good peach than on some homogeneous scrap of offensiveness picked up in the gutter. Do I quite believe in Daisy? No. Would she have run away? No. Does she interest me? Yes. Do I believe in Mr. Coward's fallen angels? Yes. Would they get drunk and deceive their husbands? Yes. Do I care if they do? No. Can *anything* they do interest me? No. Very well, then!

Let us not be too hard on that frank third-act descent to pure farce. I laughed long and loud at the ridiculously faithful waiting-room at the railway-station; at the mantelpiece like a corner of Napoleon's tomb; at the practicable train whose hootings and puffings proceeded, I felt sure, out of the multitude of Mr. Casson's personal accomplishments; at the dragonsome Pegums, particularly at her who hankered after a family vault and scorned to lie beneath common grass; at Jonty who, having imbibed too much champagne at Bee's and De Courcy's double wedding, saw in Miss Pegum a vampire learned in the secrets of the grave and, spouting Pater, went on proposing marriage till he fell backwards into the porter's truck. The piece is brilliantly played by Miss Thorndike, who is much too great an artist to insist upon always sowing with the whole sack, and gives Daisy just the right amount of significance and no more; by Miss Beatrice Smith as her double (a fine bit of wild imagination, this); by Miss Clare Greet, who would be perfect if she blacked her face and stood on her head; by Miss Winifred Oughton (a cameo of shiftlessness); by those able comedians, Messrs. Raymond Massey, Henry Caine, Arthur

Hambling, and Eliot Makeham.   Manchester, I an
told, knows all there is to be known about the
theatre.   But has it ever seen Miss Ada King in
farce ?

*May* 11.

# " Gloriana "

## A Play by GWEN JOHN

### Little Theatre

"AH, mamma, I know enough about Queen Elizabeth to know that you have left out a great many things." Thus the sententious Master Richard Markham, and thus, too, must have thought many of those who sat last Tuesday evening at the feet of Miss Gwen John. One of the most lovable, if slightly ridiculous, traits in the English character is the hankering after consistency, and the insistence that if a man is great he must also be good. Since Shakespeare was married in November his first child cannot have been born in the following May ; since Cromwell lived a plain, frugal life he cannot have had a wart upon his nose. But facts are stubborn things ; and it being impossible to deny either the wart or the date of Susanna Shakespeare's birth your romantic historian will have it, like Sentimental Tommy, that there must be a way round.

Miss John makes no apology for rewriting history. She says quite simply : " Most interpretations (of Elizabeth's personality) offered by historians are, to my

mind, so beside the mark as to be impossible." Not
only the interpretations, but also, one suggests, the facts
upon which the historians have based these interpretations. In this play Miss John has done for Elizabeth
what a playwright before her did for Mary Stuart, whose
character as drawn by Mr. Drinkwater would have
done equally well for Lady Jane Grey. The woman
who exactly three months and six days after the murder
of her husband became the wife of his murderer was
shown as a sublime creature desiring only " to see strong
children about me, to play with an easy festival mind,
to walk the evenings at peace." The great Queen who
put her rival to death out of personal hatred and jealousy,
after failing to persuade Sir Amias Paulet to do away
with her quietly—which the " dainty, precise fellow "
declined to do—this astute politician and crafty, intrigu-
ing sovereign becomes a benevolent *châtelaine* who
would have been welcomed at the tea parties of
Cranford.

Historians of all shades of opinion are agreed that
there was a great deal more " to " the mental make-up
of Elizabeth. It has been finely said that the saving
salt of her character, with all its mingled heroism and
egotism, meanness and magnificence, was that over-
much as she loved herself she loved England better.
Elizabeth was a great protestant, a great law-giver, and
a great Empire-builder, so much so that the England
which we know to-day may be said to date from her
accession. Elizabeth was more than a great Queen ;
she was a great public servant. One would willingly

admit that measured in the scale of English welfare the private blemishes of such a character weigh little, but that is a very different thing from suggesting that they do not exist. The point is an old one. Mr. Drinkwater claims that the dramatist is entitled to take or reject such elements of character as he chooses, that to omit to show historical characters as some things that they were is of no consequence, that falsification only occurs when they are shown to be something which they were not. I totally disagree. To suppress something of the truth about any character must, I submit, always falsify the portrait. Let us examine where the falsifications are in this piece. The first scene shows the Princess Elizabeth confined in the Tower, turning the pages of a missal, and confessing to her gentlewomen that she could desire to be a nun. The third scene shows her on the evening of Coronation Day exchanging sentimentalities with Mrs. Ashley and telling her that one should never sign a death-warrant because of the pleasure one might get out of it. Thus in the matter of the Queen's state of singleness Miss John would wipe away all modern views in favour of one purely sentimental—reinforced by a note in the preface, "She seems to me to have been a mystic "—and in the matter of the murdered Queen to advance the theory of pure political expediency. Better, I suggest to have told us that that same Mrs. Ashley had been committed to the Tower for conniving at Seymour's boisterous courtship of the Princess and "my lady Elizabeth's going in a night in a barge upon Thames

and for other light parts." Better to have shown
Elizabeth haggling over the responsibility for the one
great blot upon her reign. Better to have shown this
high-stomached woman falling on her knees upon hearing of her sister's death, giving thanks in good round
Latin, and rising to order the Church Service to be
read in English. One portrait shows the pale, improbable effigy ; the other the complete woman.

The greater part of this play is given over to long
scenes in which the Queen chops logic with her
Ministers on the subject of her marriage, listens to
Drake's account of the Armada, and prepares for death,
fingering a sword which, from the way she fondles it,
might have belonged to Essex or to Leicester. But the
mind goes back to the termagant and the shrew, to the
hard, imperious woman who was as vain as a peacock,
swore like a trooper, punned like H. J. Byron, and could
go to hear a sermon attended by a thousand soldiers, ten
great cannons, morris-dancers, and two white bears in a
cart. One thinks not only of the Great Queen, but of
the raddled beauty whose fair hair—she was fifty-nine
at the time and wore a red wig—Raleigh unblushingly
declared to " blow about her pure cheeks like a nymph."
Wonder at this great figure is diminished when we are
shown only one of its sides, though that side be the best.
Consistency dwarfs nature to some little scale of hill and
plain, discrepancy enables us to measure the mountain
by the ravine. I like to think of Elizabeth with her
hooked nose, black teeth, and face bedizened like Mrs.
Skewton's, murmuring " pink cushions for doctors."

But to think also of the great spirit and those last immortal words.

Miss John's dignified play is written in good nervous English, is beautifully dressed and sufficiently well acted. Miss Nancy Price plays the Queen as Duse would doubtless have played it, though with some commendable stiffening here and there. As there is not the faintest suggestion in the text that Elizabeth could ever have felt or thought or said anything which the Misses Pinkerton would have considered inadmissible, it is very clever of the actress to suggest so unmistakably that we are in the presence of a mind functioning before the age of namby-pamby. Mr. Tristan Rawson as Leicester looked very handsome and bore himself very well, but that character also was drawn too free from guile. Only Mr. Sam Livesey, as Drake, made me feel that he was anything like real. For the play, though a grave and edifying picture of what Elizabeth may have been like in her best Court mood, contains no hint of the tantrums and tornados which blew through that gusty spirit.

*December 8.*

# "The Green Hat"

## A Play by MICHAEL ARLEN

### Adelphi Theatre

TO one who is unversed in Mr. Arlen's novel Iris Fenwick, *née* March, would appear to be an exorbitant creature in all the meanings of that word. Exorbitant both in her unusualness and in the demands she makes upon life. In the beginning she was in love with Napier Harpenden, who adored and would have married her had not his father, the Major-General, forbidden a Harpenden of his line to marry into the degenerate family of March. (How lovingly and diligently Mr. Arlen pursues the county " note " !) What, now, does Iris do ? We are not living in the Middle Ages, and presumably she can go to her lover. And Napier ? Presumably the man can work for a living ; even a Harpenden should have hands. Mr. Arlen treats the weak fellow credibly and makes him do just nothing.

But Iris ? Well, she straightway becomes a wanton, and when her brother throws wantonness in her face shrugs her pretty shoulders as much as to ask what else he expects. This being a play for West End stalls, vice must not be dreary, and we are given to understand that the life led by Iris at the Continental spas is enormously expensive. Almost the implication is that it ceases to be immoral, in the way that the mistresses of French Kings imposed themselves through circumstances and pomp. Ultimately, Iris becomes the *grande amoureuse*, extenuating frailty by prodigies of gumptionless self-sacrifice. She, whose body " burns for love," marries a man to whom she is totally indifferent out of the redemptive charity and pure gold of her nature. For though Iris's body be maculate, we are to understand that her soul is unspotted. Alas, that on the night of the wedding her husband, who as a Rugger Blue has acquired the reputation of a Galahad, should throw himself out of the hotel window !

In the last act we are to learn that Fenwick is the victim of folly hitherto unsuspected, and that his suicide is a gesture of self-loathing. But for the present a further shoulder in the mountain of Iris's generosity conceals the unpleasant fact. To protect the memory of the husband she did not love, and to spare the feelings of her brother who idolised the dead man, Iris proclaims that Fenwick killed himself out of hatred of her own evil past ! She brings the curtain down on the first act declaring that what she wants henceforth is decency, and that England holds not that virtue. Ten years are now spent by the young woman careering in canary-coloured motor-cars between Deauville and Nice, her brother taking this time to kill himself with drink, and Napier using it to get engaged. The second act opens on the eve of Napier's marriage with a charming girl. Iris has returned to London ostensibly to soothe her brother's deathbed, actually to seduce Napier. This she does. The third act finds her in a French convent dying from the effects of child-birth, and restored to health by the sight of—the reader will never guess— Napier's wife !

In the fourth act our heroine turns up in England again, and Mr. Arlen takes occasion to give her a trouncing, the Major-General serving as intermediary. " We Harpendens were born in Harpendenshire ; we are part of the land. You, Iris, are an interloper. Your family was not born here. Your boundaries do not march with ours." And so on and so forth. Stung by this, Iris gives the General her dead husband's medical history. He was one of the Harpenden lot, she says, and that did not prevent his contracting syphilis. Whereupon the General collapses, and Iris proposes to carry Napier off to Buenos Aires. But just outside the front door she achieves her last height by sending Napier back to his wife with the fib that she in her turn is going to have a baby. Then she drives her motor-car head-on against the nearest tree. Is there a fifth act ? No. Sublimity's peak has been scaled.

So far from having the moral force of *Ghosts* or *Damaged Goods*, this piece has no significance of any kind. It does not point out the folly of a pair of lovers who could have bought happiness at the cost of becoming invoice clerk and shorthand typist. It does not show that the nett result of balancing a lust for self-sacrifice against unbridled appetite is that you will run full tilt into a tree. What this piece does is to take the spectator into an over-nourished, over-dressed, over-laundered, and over-sexed world, exhibit a heroine who is equally sensual and witless, and invite us to consider whether the combination does not make her really rather a darling. There can be no objection to showing sensuality for what it is ; the thing has a place in the world and in art. It is the attempt to gild sensuality with the trumperies of sham generosity which is objectionable. Also I take it that Mr. Arlen's metamorphosis is wrong in fact. Lady into fox may be thinkable ; vixen into goose is absurd. These people have no occupation save making love, if love be the word ; and one would say that their world is like a deer forest in the rutting season, if it were not that the stag is a noble animal. Everybody talks too much of " cleanliness " and " purity," states which normal beings take for granted. The author has apparently not learned enough of English ways to know that a man does not go about prating of his friend as " the cleanest chap on earth," and that unmarried ladies do not allude to themselves publicly as virgins. But it is when the author sermonises that we believe him least. He writes half-heartedly between the lines, and we can read through them.

In all fairness, it must be added that the play was not dull ; the tale was alternately vicious and silly, but in three out of the four acts there was plenty of vigour in the telling. The acting was good throughout, and in the case of Mr. Eric Maturin as the degenerate brother, superb. There was a demoniac power here which it did one good to see. Miss Tallulah Bankhead brought all her husky charm to the part of Iris, and acted pleasantly and competently without making one feel that the character could have moved in any mentionable society. Mr. Norman McKinnel as the General was duly dour and uncompromising. Mr. Frederick Leister conveyed admirably the Doctor's disgust at having to descend into this underbred world, and Mr. Leonard Upton wore Napier Harpenden's morals and clothes with admirable assurance. Mr. Julian Royce trailed behind him the clouds of all Pinero's *raisonneurs* rolled into one. To see Hilary Townshend drink whisky, smoke a cigar, and hear him enunciate a platitude was to meet that innocent worldling, Cayley Drummle, in apotheosis.

*September 2.*

# "Fallen Angels"

A Comedy by NOËL COWARD

Globe Theatre

# "Ariadne, or Business First"

A Comedy by A. A. MILNE

Haymarket Theatre

He thought he saw a giddy goat
　　Advance by three and three ;
He looked again, and saw it was
　　A brilliant repartee.
" How doth—how surely doth," he said,
　" The little busy bee."

Nonsense Rhyme.

THIS trifling, foolish verse came into my head
as soon as Ariadne started quoting from her
book on bee-keeping. (Was it Avebury or Maeter-
linck ? But the point is immaterial.) Both these
comedies, looked at the morning after, boil down to that
question of repartee. Was there enough grace in the

dialogue to redeem them ?   Both authors had obviously been busy as bees gathering the honey of their quips from two entirely different cultures—flowers of evil in the Baudelairian sense and blossoms of the goody-goody.

Mr. Coward is a very young playwright—of quite extraordinary gifts, to which I shall come later on—who at the moment can no more be trusted with his talent for playwriting than a schoolboy can be trusted who has stolen a piece of chalk and encounters a providentially blank wall.   Where his angels have originally tumbled from I have no notion, nor probably has Mr. Coward.   The important thing for him is that they are now in the dirt, and that he can spend three hours well and truly rubbing their noses in that dirt.   And ours too.   By the end of the evening the air of the theatre was rank with stale patchouli.   No, I am wrong.   Patchouli, when it was the mode, was at least an honest scent ; you knew its users for the good Cyprians that they were.   Whereas these drunken ladies, dwelling luxuriously on their provokingly delayed " fall," doubtless thought themselves a cut above *that*, and many cuts above the parlour-maid whose shoes they were obviously unworthy to black.

" This is not a court of morals," is a pronouncement frequently made by the judicial bench, and it is possible that Mr. Coward might put up that plea for his beloved theatre.   Indeed, I would rather be briefed for the easier case of light-hearted defence than that of heavy-handed attack.   What about the Palais Royal farces of

135

immemorial sanction and the present licence of Sacha Guitry ? What about the laughing castigation of manners and the lawful scarifying of the times ? Do we hold our nose at Wycherley ? Or, come to that, at Maugham ? These are posers which have to be answered. Mr. Coward has admitted that he was tempted to write a French comedy in the English language—which seems to me to be as senseless a proceeding as to try to write an English comedy in the French language. A rose in another tongue may not smell by any means as sweet, and your Latin well of truth turns easily into your Saxon cesspool. It is no use discussing *why* this should be so. It *is* so, and that's all there is to be said for the French defence. On the English score Wycherley may be dirt, but at least he is honest dirt, with the compensation of rude vigour and immense vitality. *Fallen Angels* glitters with the phosphorescence of decay. Mr. Maugham ? Well, in *Our Betters* Mr. Maugham set a bad example supremely well, and perhaps the example was not so bad after all. That decent American boy and girl were of immense value : they stood for the background of sanity against which the demented exposed their dementia.

But Mr. Coward's characters have neither virility nor life. In none of his plays has he yet drawn a man, and the women in this one possess not vitality but "headiness" in the champagne sense. And the normal background which Mr. Maugham was so careful to present is simply not there. The husbands are neither

men nor golfers, but numskulls so completely null that
whether they are decent or not doesn't matter.   Now
let us admit that the business of dramatic art, as of any
other kind, is not to do good by direct moral precept but
to invigorate the imagination, and so point the way to
health.   Mr. Coward's art transgresses this rule.   It is
purely enervating, and the atmosphere is that of the
hot-house whose blooms are essentially *fleurs du mal.*

But even the youngest and most disquieting playwright must be given his due.   One's gorge did not
rise, I repeat, till the day after, the throat being fully
occupied with the immediate business of laughter.   For
the play really *was* funny, and the dialogue as good as
any that has been heard in the theatre since Wilde.
Only it was just not good enough to drown enormity.
The technics of the play as a piece of cabinet-making
were almost beyond reproach, and now that I have
used the word I suggest that it be used not too intem-
perately.   The extravaganza—for that is what this
play really is—shows not a nasty mind, but a juvenile
preoccupation with nasty things common to some
young people at the age of puberty.   They grow out
of it, and if Mr. Coward has the sense with which I
credit him, so will he.   At present he reminds me of a
line in another nonsense verse :—

While round and round
The rapid whiting, tail in mouth, shall whirl
In ever-widening rings.

Mr. Coward is too rapid, his tongue is too constantly in his
cheek, and the circle of his characters is not wide enough.

On the other hand, Mr. Milne's characters are like caged dormice, putting from time to time a passionless paw into the outer world and drawing it back again. One quickly tires of these Ariadnes and Evadnes, Belindas and Lucindas. A single act of them is a delight; the rest is tedium. If only Mr. Milne and Mr. Coward would exchange worlds for a while! Or if both would take a ride together on a 'bus going Bermondsey way and have a look at the working man, or Brixton way and see what the great bulk of middle-class people look and talk like! Life is not, as these two seem to think, either all night-club or all potting-shed. Incidentally each has got the visible surface of the world postulated all wrong. The wives of golfing stockbrokers do not wear hundred-guinea dinner-gowns from the Rue St. Honoré. Provincial solicitors do not have drawing-rooms of the dreamy and creamy exquisiteness of the one in Ariadne's house at Melchester. (Where have I heard that name before?) Nor has Mr. Milne actually encountered his vulgarian. The Horace Meldrums of this world, in receipt of a thousand a week, do not put off a fascinating adventure for the sake of a business engagement worth a paltry hundred. They are much more likely to pay the price of vanity, fully intending to make capital out of it with the lady afterwards. As usual, Mr. Milne lacks the courage of his first act. What we want to see is how Ariadne will behave at the clandestine lunch. What we get is the reason why it does not take place.

If Mr. Milne's fault is one of omission, Mr. Coward

makes the opposite mistake. Why show the Frenchman who can only disappoint ? He could leave the
scenes of the wives' mutual inculpation and exculpation.
But, then, let the bell ring and the maid announce the
long-expected conquering hero. And, just as he is
about to enter, *curtain !* What missed chance was
here !

The acting in both pieces was superb. All praise
to Miss Best, who overcame with complete triumph the
handicap of natural modesty, and to Miss Bankhead,
impersonating to the life a joyless creature whose
spiritual home was the gutter. Miss Compton heaped
mountainous charm on molehill incident, Mr. Aynesworth magnoperated, and Mr. Deverell played the fool
with genius.

*April* 21, 22.

# " Spring  Cleaning "

## A COMEDY BY FREDERICK LONSDALE

### ST. MARTIN'S THEATRE

THIS is easily the best play of a good week. It is all nonsense to pretend that a fine dinner is essential to the enjoyment of a fine play, and that what is in a dramatist's head is conditioned by what is in his audience's stomach. Owing to a series of accidents and fear of Mr. Dean's Draconian law I saw this play in a foodless condition. But I enjoyed every moment of it, and at the end was faint with pleasure rather than from inanition.

Our vicious children are not likely to be spoilt for lack of the rod. Mr. Coward came recently to the support of Mr. Maugham's flagellant arm, and Mr. Arlen would have done likewise had he not sympathised too much with the offenders. Mr. Lonsdale lays about him in scarifying fashion, but it would not altogether surprise me if his victims enjoy it as much as anybody. Backs may be scarred with little effect on the withers. But Mr. Lonsdale is an intelligent chastiser, and knowing that satire should fall equally on the would-be just as upon the conscientiously unjust has a few choice scorpions left over for the plaguing of virtue's standard-bearer.

He sees that good Richard Sones is a bore, and that the life of poor Margaret Sones cannot be entirely filled by looking after her two children and poring over the scenarios of her husband's novels. He sees, too, that the crowd of pleasure-seekers really does find what it seeks ; and he avoids the fatuous delusion of the unco' guid that absinthe before dinner spells misery for the rest of that evening and in the life to come as well. He sees again that the husband is a fool, or he need not have resorted to the extreme outrage of introducing Mona, that wreckage of the pavement, to the dinner-table of his wife and her guests.

But I am not quite sure whether Mr. Lonsdale realises that the outrage is really committed upon poor Mona, who would hardly, I submit, have " stood for " the object-lesson. The situation is not entirely credible, but Mr. Lonsdale manages it very well, and his *courtisane* ratiocinates as little as may be. Some day a playwright will present us with a street-walker who is not a perambulating fountain of philosophy and charitableness, but that day is not yet. The last act, in which the would-be lover turns friend of the family, is a marvel of good writing, but all through the craftsmanship is excellent, and the result is one shimmer of sustained brilliance.

Everybody will be asking how the play compares

with *The Vortex*. (*Our Betters* is in a class by itself.) In one way it is an improvement, for it is not marred by the sentimental assumptions of Mr. Coward's last act. In another it is not so good, in so far as we are not in the presence of quite so subtle a mind. But subtlety is the enemy of punch, and of punch this play has enough and to spare. It is an admirable piece of pure theatre, and as such could be enjoyed before breakfast.

The acting is excellent throughout. Miss Cecily Byrne is very right after her catastrophic dinner-party, but I think that earlier on she should be slightly ridiculous. Good little bourgeoise that she is, she should ape the fantastic manners of her invaders, none of whom would otherwise trouble to visit her. Except, of course, for her dinners. Mr. Ian Hunter and Mr. Ronald Squire are quite perfect throughout, and that immensely improving actress, Miss Edna Best, makes a tiny part into a thing of beauty. Miss Cathleen Nesbitt's Mona never falters, and the actress serves her author well. I do not quite know how Mr. Denys Blakelock is going to fortify his soul against the ravages of his "fairy." Perhaps he should now play a plumber by way of antidote. In the meantime he gets shouts of laughter.

Mr. Harris's settings are superb. But would it not be possible to arrange some scheme of lighting whereby the gorgeousness of rooms, once it has gone home to the beholders, should not remain quite so insistent? The actors in this play do not stand out quite so much as they should from the riot of cushions, curtains, upholstery, and carpets.   But Margaret's dining-room is undeniably exquisite.

*January* 29.

# "The Last of Mrs. Cheyney"

## A Play by FREDERICK LONSDALE

### St. James's Theatre

. . . popular preference for fun, fashionable dresses, a little music, and even an exhibition of eating and drinking by people with an expensive air.—BERNARD SHAW.

The world is still deceived with ornament.—SHAKESPEARE.

FINE feathers make fine birds, and fine birds make fine plays, or at least paying "propositions." Countless plays have proved beyond shadow of doubt the managerial contention that the number of playgoers in London alive to and immediately curious about the intellectual theatre is at the most forty thousand, and may be very much less. But take forty thousand from seven millions and a considerable balance remains, to entertain which is a complicated business. The complications are lessened as soon as the playwright realises that the West End audience takes no interest in low life except on condition that it is above stairs. Mr. Lonsdale owes his success to his perfect realisation of this fact. There is no secret about successful playwriting. Avoidance of any kind of truth, wit which does not rise out of character but is an impartial distribution from the author's private storehouse, and, as to players, stars of whoppingest magnitude with no nonsense about team work—this cannot be wrong. The success of *The Last of Mrs. Cheyney* will, I imagine, be found to correspond exactly with the faithful carrying-out of this formula. It is not a good sort of play, but it is a very good play of its sort.

Mr. Lonsdale's curtain rises on a gilded saloon, giving on to the garden in which vicious owners of the land are entertaining the virtuous tillers thereof. Presently Mr. Ronald Squire enters disguised as a butler, yet cinct and girt with an Oxford manner. To him comes an indefatigably inquisitive young footman, to whom Charles explains that their mistress's guests must be the best people since they have the worst manners. And now the garden party draws to a close—there are to be no fireworks, since Charles has let them all off within doors. The characters enter in inverse order of significance, like an England batting team which should go in tail first. They, too, coruscate. There are two lords, one of whom is an old fool, the other a debonair drunkard. Which will Mrs. Cheyney prefer —the rent-roll or the *mauvais garçon ?* And then the scene changes. The shades of eve have fallen fast, the eldest villager has bent his last sad spectral hairs, the nobility has gone to dress for dinner, leaving the world to darkness and Mrs. Cheyney, her piano and Scriabin.

The first footman enters, and, having drawn the curtains with ceremony, produces from his pocket a packet of " fags," one of which he " puts on." The lady continues to address herself to Scriabin. The second footman and the chauffeur enter and sit about at their ease. Still no rebuke from the piano. Finally, Charles enters, smoking an admirable cigar. The first footman, weary of Scriabin, comes straight to the point : " What about them pearls ? " (It used to be " sparklers," but other times other jewels.) Mrs. Cheyney is a crook counting major-domo and vassalage her accomplices. She says she is " getting warm." The under-footman calls for a livelier tune, and foots it as the curtain descends to the thumping of " I Want to be Happy."

All this has been very good, but from this point the play, as a piece of nature or observation, goes steadily to pieces. And this because the author must needs forsake the primrose path of pearl-snatching for the steep and thorny road of popular psychology. Or let us say heart-interest, the gateway of popular taste. Who, after a good dinner, could doubt that a thief clever enough to know real pearls from imitation will know quite perfectly the value of the jewel locked in her own breast ? Who, when the *mauvais garçon* offered the lady choice between five years in gaol and a night of gallantry, could doubt again that she would throw the rest of the champagne into Quex's face and ring Sophy Fulgarney's bell ? Or that upon the entry of the awakened household the pair would exchange prodigies of gumptionless self-sacrifice ? It would seem now

that there is nothing to save the poor girl from gaol.
But stay ! We learn at next morning's breakfast table
—the board at which high society adjudicates upon the
events of the night before—that the stupid lord has
written a letter to Mrs. Cheyney in which he not only
proposes marriage, but gives away the character of
every member of the house-party. If they prosecute,
the woman will, or so we are told, produce the letter
in court and make everybody ridiculous. Whereupon
everybody invites blackmail, and finally thrusts freedom,
a ticket for Australia, and ten thousand pounds upon
the blackmailer. But Mrs. Cheyney has yet another
jewel up her sleeve—her love for the rascal who bade
her ring upon the bell. She tears up the cheque as, she
now confesses, she has torn up the letter of which no
honourable thief could possibly make use. The
cricket team slinks back into the pavilion, and the thief
falls into the noble toper's arms. We leave the theatre
reflecting that though Hamlet could not bear to look
upon Ophelia as a breeder of sinners, our hero must be a
manlier fellow in that he looks forward without dismay
to becoming the founder of a race of pickpockets and
dipsomaniacs.

The cast was made up of fashionable players, each of
whom, finding nothing human to act, proceeded to give
an impersonation of a familiar self at its greatest point
of superbity, nonchalance, and what not. Thus Sir
Gerald du Maurier flaunted his old impenitent grace,
Miss Gladys Cooper aired her practised elegance, Mr.
Ronald Squire fired off the Roman candles of his

punctilious wit, Mr. Basil Loder edited a whole volume of bucolics, Dame May Whitty gave her exposition of mothering, and Miss Ellis Jeffreys soared into the empyrean of her own technique. The whole thing was a marvel of timing, and as much a miracle of getting out of each other's way as cab-driving in the Strand on a Saturday night. One piece of indifferent acting came from that very distinguished artist, Mr. Dawson Milward. Indifferent, because Mr. Milward never persuaded me for a moment that he was really stupid. He simulated the outward semblance of all that is crass but not the core. If, however, to have suggested the possibility of gentleness in such surroundings was to be successful, then Mr. Milward scored a great triumph. But the best performance of all seemed to me to be the junior footman of Mr. Frank Lawton. The London streets are full of *gamins* who have put on astonishment with their first livery, whereas I have never to my knowledge set eyes on any of Mr. Lonsdale's pearl-wearers and pearl-snatchers. I suggest *Thomas in Wonderland* as an alternative title. The house, having taken the measure of the bulge in Mr. Lonsdale's cheek, enjoyed itself famously.

*September* 22.

# " Hay Fever "

A Comedy by NOËL COWARD

Ambassadors Theatre

CHARLES DICKENS is very much in the air
these days. When Mr. Ashley Dukes
proposed the health of the dramatists at the annual
dinner of the Critics' Circle the other evening he
alluded to that " greatest of Victorian dramatists who
had never written a play." And Mr. Dukes was right
in his implied criticism, for almost the whole of Dickens
is sheer drama, and it is a great pity that plays of the
present day do not possess more of the spirit of that great
writer.

Every country has longed to possess a Dickens. We
sometimes hear Balzac alluded to as the French
Dickens, while only the other day there was a profound
article in a high-brow weekly seeking to establish the
fact that Tchehov was the Russian Charles. English
playwriting has either advanced a long way ahead of our
great novelist, or it has receded a long way behind ; and
probably the nearest approach to that master on the
English stage is to be found in the " sob-stuff " of the
American sentimental comedy and the Los Angeles

film. Dickens, you see, was not afraid of the human emotions, which skeer to death the advanced playwrights of the English stage. Leaving aside the author of *The Silver Box*, who at his best is pure Dickens and at his second-best is pure Galsworthy, what writer have we at the present day who will so far bemean himself as to condescend to the feelings ? Mr. Maugham ? Personally, I take that brilliant and cynical writer to be entirely heartless, and it is to be remembered that the piece in which Sadie Thompson wrings our heart with the baring of her vulgar little bosom is only the adaptation of a work which the writer was careful to conceive in the form of a short story. Mr. Frederick Lonsdale ? In my humble view, the amount of genuine emotion in *Spring Cleaning* was less than the sympathy felt by the alleged ladies in that piece for the woman of the streets who insisted upon that title, or, alternatively, than the amount of respect felt by the professional for the amateur.

Let me say that I am not including in my list of playwrights Sir James Barrie, Mr. Shaw, Mr. Henry Arthur Jones, or any of the great and acknowledged war-horses, nor even your modern intellectual playwrights like Mr. Ashley Dukes, whose *Man with a Load of Mischief* is full of emotion of the purely æsthetic sort. I am thinking of the " smart " young writers whose work it is " the thing " to see and, if you be equally young and smart, to marvel at. A typical playwright of this sort is Mr. Noël Coward, who at the moment has four plays running in the town, and all of them as barren of emotion as a moneylender is of generosity. *The Vortex* has a certain quality of hectic excitement which may make the galled Society jade wince, but will not wring the withers of the man in the street. Comparatively few of us, after all, possess mothers who go off with their son's sweetheart's discarded lover. It is not to be imagined that if Mr. Noël Coward's Queen Gertrude and her precious son, Hamlet, were drowned in a bucket of disinfectant—a consummation devoutly to be wished—it is not thinkable that in the course of three hundred performances one single tear would be dropped. Charles Lamb declared that if one of Congreve's or Wycherley's personages were placed in a modern play his virtuous indignation "shall rise against the profligate wretch as warmly as the Catos of the pit could desire." Why does not our virtuous indignation rise against these two profligate madams in *Fallen Angels*, seeing that they are placed in a modern play where we are supposed to judge of the right and the wrong? The reason is because neither creature has ever had, or ever could have, an emotion, their sentimental peripatetics being dictated solely by appetite. We are certain that our wives, mothers, sisters, and daughters are not made in this mould, and we are as much amused and as little touched as if the spectacle were that of a Hottentot *ménage*.

It is not denied that in the concoction of trivialities Mr. Coward cannot be excelled. But the point I want to make is that the English theatre, or rather that part of it which has its home in Shaftesbury Avenue, is in process of starvation. The average playgoer cried out for the bread of emotion, and Mr. Coward offers him a Noëlism. His new piece of unpretentious fooling is a *moue* made at those of his mentors who insist that he shall grow up into a writer of "serious" plays. Not that *The Vortex* hadn't a moral. It had. It had lots of morals, sufficient in any case to make you feel that the writer had dabbled in low things out of the highest motives. Was there an uneasy suspicion that after all her son's haranguing the mother would backslide? *Tant pis ;* and in any case we reflected that there was precedent, since in the moral play of *Hamlet* the Queen seems to have gone back on her midnight resolution long before the day of the duelling. Then came *Fallen Angels*, and the case for the author as scourger of modern manners seemed pretty thin. Wasn't the naughty part of it done with too much relish?

After the curtain had fallen upon *Hay Fever*, Mr. Coward came forward and said that though we might have found the piece excessively dreary we must admit that it was as clean as a whistle. I beg to take exceptions to both halves of this statement. The piece is by no means dreary, and I am not to be cajoled into mistaking anæmia for morality. There is neither health nor cleanness about any of Mr. Coward's characters, who are still the same vicious babies sprawling upon the floor of their unwholesome *crèche*. Take any one of the characters you like. Take the boy Simon. His mother regrets that he cannot be taught to box—" he's so dreadfully un—that sort of thing." He is helpless on the river, thanks God that his sister is not " a fresh, open-air girl with a passion for games," abuses the word " marvellous," and when they want an adverb for a guessing-competition suggests " winsomely." The mother, Judith, spends the afternoon, in the words of a visitor, " bouncing about on the sofa with a hearty young thing in flannels," and is capable of warning her daughter that because she is a vigorous *ingénue* of nineteen she is not to expect a monopoly of amorous adventure. Are there such mothers ? Does any one of the characters exist ?

But it would be foolish to insist upon attacking this play on the score of truth or morality. Mr. Coward began it, as they say, with his talk of whistles. But even a whistle has to exist before it can be either " convincing "—if Mr. Walkley will allow me to use that detested word—or clean. There is no theme here to be either moral or immoral. As a piece of brilliant, impudent, and sustained fooling the play is very pleasant entertainment, and well enough " made " to delight a Frenchman. The ex-actress who cannot have an emotion without merging it in one of her old parts or the more dithyrambic passages of her husband's vile novels, the quartet of week-end visitors who flirt with anybody except the person they were invited down to the country cottage to flirt with—all this is excellent.

And then there is the dialogue, for which Mr. Coward's simile would be much more apt. This is clean indeed, in the sense that it is whittled and pared to an admirable fineness. Take that passage in which two visitors, having arrived together, find themselves alone and neglected.   It should be said that Jackie is a girl :—

> JACKIE : Have you travelled a lot ?
> RICHARD (*modestly*) : A good deal.
> JACKIE : How lovely.
> > *There is a pause.*
> RICHARD : Spain is very beautiful.
> JACKIE : Yes, I've always heard Spain was awfully nice.
> RICHARD : Except for the bull-fights.   No one who ever really loved horses would enjoy a bull-fight.
> JACKIE : Nor any one who loved bulls either.
> RICHARD : Exactly.
> JACKIE : Italy's awfully nice, isn't it ?
> RICHARD : Oh, yes, charming.
> JACKIE : I've always wanted to go to Italy.
> RICHARD : Rome is a beautiful city.
> JACKIE : Yes, I've always heard Rome was lovely .
> RICHARD : Have you ever been abroad at all ?
> JACKIE : Oh, yes ; I went to Dieppe once— we had a house there for the summer.
> RICHARD (*kindly*) : Dear little place—Dieppe.
> JACKIE : Yes, it was lovely.
> RICHARD : Russia used to be a wonderful place before the war, etc., etc.

I venture to suggest that many moral plays are not enlivened with such delicate imbecility.   On this score at least, my heartiest congratulations.   Mr. Coward is credited with the capacity to turn out these very highly polished pieces of writing in an incredibly short time.

And if rumour and the illustrated weeklies are to be believed, he writes his plays in a flowered dressing-gown and before breakfast. But what I want to know is what kind of work he intends to do after breakfast, when he is clothed and in his right mind.

I want to make two points here. The first is that the nursery vein is a thin one, and there are signs in the present play that for this writer it is almost worked out. It has been said that the characters in *Hay Fever* are Tchehovian. They are, but with a difference. Those Russian maunderers and drivellers lie back in their cherry orchard mouthing grandiose futilities at the stars ; these English ones sprawl on their stomachs wittily picking the nursery hearthrug to pieces. Let their author stick to his rod, but let him spare us more of these silly children. My second point is that such plays are bad for the theatre. They appeal to an infinitesimally small and, I believe, purely Metropolitan audience. Their success is one almost entirely of curiosity, even of a more or less prurient itch from which the country as a whole is free. Your good dramatist is welcome on Humber as on Thames. Will Mr. Coward risk a fall with Hull ? All the provincial managers are crying out against the " sex-play." Will not Mr. Coward see to it in the future that he has something to say to the country as well as the town ? My advice to him is to forget all about that which he vaguely deems to be " Society," and to go down to Southend and spend a week amongst dead winkles and people who are really alive, and to sprawl on the beach with any novel by Charles Dickens. Let this playwright forget that genius has been attributed to him in the portrayal of those classes about whom nobody cares anything at all, and let him show us whether he has the talent to depict people who really exist. It was a capital mistake to come forward and say, as he virtually did say, " You tell me I can't write a clean comedy. Well, here is a clean comedy, as clean as a whistle, and see how little inspiration I find in cleanliness ! "

The piece was played a great deal better than it deserved by Miss Marie Tempest and her company. Miss Tempest has, I understand, been out of England for a considerable period, and she would do well to get some woman to tell her what kind of frocks are worn during week-ends in this country.

*June* 8.

# " Rain "

A Play Adapted from the Novel of W. Somerset
Maugham

By JOHN COLTON and CLEMENCE
RANDOLPH

Garrick Theatre

MESSRS. REANDEAN, like your cheerful
vendors of umbrellas, have never ceased to
assure us that we should have " Rain." The long-
promised downpour took place on Tuesday evening,
and proved a very handsome affair. Rather too handsome, perhaps, for the sworn devotees of Mr. Maugham,
but altogether satisfactory to any remaining this side of
that distinguished pale. Such exceptions saw justice
done, roughly, perhaps, but on the whole satisfactorily,
and poetically to this extent that the trouncing of the
unco' guid was accomplished by sanctimony's victim.
The moral was two-fold : first, that some kinds of
goodness cause more unhappiness than some kinds of
evil ; second, that people without sin would do better
to refrain from throwing stones. Which propositions
combine in the theatre to form an unction lenitive,
balsamic, and altogether flattering to the natural man's

sense of the fair and the proper. It is fair that soiled doves should come to rest on rugged, protective bosoms, and proper that self-appointed judges should be incapacitated from judging further. Therefore was it that when Sadie Thompson threw her arms round Sergeant O'Hara's neck within five seconds of hearing that her would-be converter had killed himself because of his love for her—therefore the audience drew a long breath of relief, cheered the girl to the echo, and deemed the missionary's end " good riddance of bad rubbish."

But is that quite Mr. Maugham's story ? I am not going to insist upon mechanical defects. Obviously there was not enough material in the tale for a full-length play, but against this we must set the fact that the padding was the very best possible, and that the third act was extremely fine. What was important was the shifting of interest from confessor to penitent. This was bound to happen, and the adapters can hardly be blamed. The Sadie Thompsons may occupy an insignificant corner of the world's stage, but in the theatre they must hold the dead centre. This may not be a law of Nature, but it is certainly one of curiosity. Virtue, in the theatre, has hard work to appear other than the embodiment of refusal and restraint—a respectable heroine, if you like, but anæmic and Thackerayish. Whereas Vice has but to put in the tip of her meddlesome little nose, and Virtue's is at once put out.

Now present Virtue in the guise, bands, and bonds of a Calvinist missionary burning with a fire of zeal so hot that it consumes natural pity like mere dross. Give

the poor bigot words so remote from normal thinking
that his hearers can hardly believe their ears, deprive
him of any phrase in which to express his growing self-
distrust and self-loathing, show him leaping to the sin
he is most urgent to condemn, and the difficulty is not
so much that of accepting the fellow as hero as of not
mistaking him for villain. Throughout the first two
acts the audience applauded every stroke of the ironical
doctor's light cane and every thwack of Sadie's lusty
besom ; the missionary was obviously little better than
Stiggins, and the allocation of the number in Mr.
Creakle's prison next after those of Uriah Heep and
Mr. Littimer would have met the case sufficiently.
But then came that distressing and unaccountable
suicide, and with it the need for serious revision of
opinion. Hypocrites always weather exposure somehow ; this was different. The applause now was
less hearty, because no audience can press hand to brow
and at the same time clap.

Or is this to impute to the audience what one might
have felt if one had not known the story ? I believe
that for the first half I should have been prepared to dub
the play sentimental comedy, and been considerably
irked at having to make the tragic twist. As it was I
felt myself asking as each tragic clue, carefully left in
by the adapters, came round : Should I have spotted
this ? Should I have detected the significance of the
missionary's preoccupation on his first entry, of those
allusions to his sleeplessness and nocturnal perambula-
tions ? It may be that everybody in the house saw

which hare Mr. Maugham originally pursued ; saw,
too, that Sadie's terrific outburst at the end of the second
act was not the whole case, but only the impassioned
speech of counsel for the defence ; saw again that the
severity which the missionary meted out to Sadie would
serve his own turn, only more so ; saw finally, not only
at the last moment of the play but had seen throughout,
that here was essential tragedy, the conflict not of right
against wrong but of contending ideas of right.   If this
was generally perceived then the play is as perfect as the
story.

It is possible that the missionary was not entrusted
to the right actor, that a player would have done better
who should have been able to suggest not only stupidity,
but stupidity in incandescence.   Mr. Malcolm Keen's
profile was against him. and he looked the inquisitorial
eagle rather than the inspired gander.   No man with
that educated manner and incisive speech could possibly
have believed in the propriety of telling the South Sea
Islander that he has been living in sin since the days
of the Pterodactyl.   Mr. Keen dominated ; he should
have been possessed.   And possessed, too, with that
sublime power of unreason which shoos logic out of the
world.   You can see the kind of fanatic I mean every
evening in the Park ; as he thumps his tub madness
stares out of his face.   With such an one the philosophical doctor would have known the uselessness of argument.   Mr. J. H. Roberts didn't argue, but I was
worried that he didn't.   I felt sure that if he had taken
Mr. Keen by the arm and said, " My dear fellow, don't

you see . . . ? " the dear fellow would have seen. But given the basis of a rational instead of an irrational being, Mr. Keen's super-structure was very good indeed.

On the other hand the missionary's wife was admirably suggested. There was on her face just that look which is half-witted and half-blessed, that yonderliness of silly innocence—in the best meaning of the word " silly "—which the old painters knew so well. She was rapt indeed, had known nothing but a foolish ecstasy ever since those early days in some dingy suburb, though she had assembled about her, from goodness knows where, an air of being superficially businesslike and sane. Miss Marda Vanne invested this poor creature with extraordinary dignity and won the entire sympathy of the house, though every word of the part cut across our sensibilities like a knife. As for Miss Olga Lindo, I think I must begin by saying that she faced her very difficult job with immense pluck. Was the first part of her performance more than competent ? One thinks not. Could it have been more than competent ? Again one thinks not. Here, once more, it must be insisted that Mr. Maugham did not write his story round Sadie. Had he done so, he might well have made her the Anna Christie which she is not. Therefore it is that the adapters, making too much of Sadie, have found themselves gravelled for original matter of genius and have fallen back upon boisterousness and slang. I can think of half a dozen actresses who could have equalled Miss Lindo here, and one, at least, who could have surpassed her. But I can think of none who could have tacked on to rowdiness that scene of conversion in which the poor wretch was translated into another world. Here were beauty and pathos, a hint of the ineffable and something even of redemption. I offer Miss Lindo my very sincerest congratulations. Only an artist of a very high order could have delivered the line : " Then I forgive him " as she delivered it.

Mr. Shep Camp contributed a character-study of great art and vigour, Mr. Stuart Sage was a manly and likeable lover, and Miss Barbara Gott exasperated me as usual by her limitless perfection. The setting was fine and the rain discreet.

*May* 12.

# "The Moon and Six-pence"

### A Play Adapted from the Novel of W. Somerset Maugham by EDITH ELLIS

#### New Theatre

"APART from his genius my husband was in every way a perfectly normal man," insisted at the end of this play the wife of Charles Strickland, the painter. Whether men of genius can be normal in other respects would make a capital subject for debating societies wearied of determining whether the hangman should or should not be abolished. There are two sides to every question. Readers of my distinguished colleague, Mr. Ernest Newman, know that half the world holds that Richard Wagner, one of the most stupendous geniuses in history, was, outside his genius, rather a nasty little man, the other half being content to see in the last act of *Tristan and Isolda* proof that its composer paid his tailor regularly and never loved more than one woman at a time. The way one votes on such a question depends largely upon whether one holds the feather-bed view of human nature, and believes that bulges have to be paid for by corresponding depressions. According to this theory extraordinary genius, or super-normality, in one part of a man's being has to be accounted for by deficiency, or sub-normality, in another part. Thus your artist will pay for his artistry by failure in self-control, companionableness, charity, ordinary decency, or any one of a hundred ways.

Something of this kind has to be accepted, or we should write Strickland down pure monster. Here is an artist utterly without scruple outside his artistry, yet within that domain the perfect thrall to conscience. This stockbroker at forty abandons his wife and children, goes to Paris, steals a Good Samaritan's wife and abandons her, ekes out an existence by sponging and cadging, and at the last sails for the Islands of the Pacific Ocean there to live upon a native woman and paint pictures which the world is afterwards to recognise as masterpieces. Can such things be ? Yes, since Strickland is really Paul Gauguin. Put such things into a play and what lesson shall we deduce ? I think none, any more than we can deduce a lesson from the career of the poet Rimbaud, who did the exact opposite to Gauguin, and after having achieved immortality at seventeen abjured his art and went in for huxtering. No moral is to be drawn from such extraordinary cases, even if the business of art were to supplement the copy-book. Knowledge of these cases widens experience, and at the most teaches us that it is as foolish to put extraordinary men to ordinary tests as to measure a world of four dimensions by one of three. Is this a

good play ?   Not in Mr. Lonsdale's sense, perhaps, but
it is a very interesting one.   Two out of the six scenes
are admirable.   The piece is technically less than good
because the first scene in Mrs. Strickland's drawing-
room is entirely unnecessary ;  all that it is intended to
mean could quite easily have been conveyed by Strickland in the second scene.   In fact, that artist does convey it all—the futility of the wife who knows nothing
of her husband and cares for nothing except the position
which she derives from him.   The last scene, showing
Strickland's posthumous celebrity, is also unnecessary.
Dramatically it is an anti-climax, and we must have
already realised the greatness of the pictures and of the
artist's ultimate fame or the whole play has been
nonsense.

The piece is in six scenes.   The second, which
showed the painter ill and starving in his garret, was
full of the right kind of harshness and brutality.   So,
too, was the third scene, in which the artist trampled
beneath his feet kindness, decency, and everything that
men associate with honour.   Mr. Maugham and Mr.
Ainley between them certainly created here an artist
in whom one could believe, though the convention used
was romantic rather than realistic.   Miss Clare Harris,
who brings remarkable understanding to everything she
plays, gave an admirable rendering of the possessive
element in women's love which so irks the Stricklands.
Every artist knows how utterly he belongs to himself
and to nobody else, not even the Heavenly Choir.   This
is the one thing which the mothering type of woman

will never understand unless she is heroic enough knowingly to mother that which can never belong to her. Miss Harris had to present the passion of a stupid woman, and did it admirably. I suggest that the Good Samaritan of Mr. George Elton was altogether too maudlin a creature. After all, Dirk Stroeve was an artist, if a bad one ; and Mr. Elton did not make me feel that Stroeve could have painted his own front door. Some suggestion of temperament was wanted, some suggestion of William Schmucke, the friend of Cousin Pons.

The piece after the third scene went sadly astray, and for some half-hour we had to put up with diligent and unnecessary local colouring which we could have taken for granted. The humours of Miss Margaret Yarde's native woman and Mr. Tom Reynolds' sea-captain were considerable successes in their way, but the play hereabouts was on a definitely low level. Here also we were introduced to the native and rather pinch-beck enchantress of Miss Eileen Sharp who, if her complexion had been a shade lighter, would not have seemed out of place as a leader in the Girl Guides. Mr. Ainley, too, had lost all his admirable brusqueness, though one should perhaps take into account the fact that Papeete, like Bournemouth, is relaxing. The fifth scene was devoted to the doctor's revelation to the artist of the dread approach of leprosy. Here Mr. Ainley achieved considerable pathos, but one felt that so good an actor could have ennobled similarly a page of Edna Lyall. If this scene had been on the level of the second and third Strickland would have fallen to cursing instead of attitudinising, and the doctor would have called for water to wash his hands. But here Miss Eileen Sharp acted very much better, and it would be churlish not to recognise some kind of merit in a situation which certainly held the house. But the better was ever the enemy of the good, and I repeat that the second and third scenes were good enough to make a sorry mess of the subsequent sentimentalities. Let it be said that Mr. Ainley always acted up to the height of his authors' intentions, and sometimes soared a good deal beyond them.

There shall be no serious attempt to apportion high praise for the good things and blame for the poorer ones. Perhaps one does not easily associate Mr. Maugham with such infant witticism as " delirium trimmings," or such a tag of philosophy as " Life, how strange and dreadful it is ! " But let these pass. The dialogue in the best scenes was taut and spare as a barrel. Mr. Reginald Denham produced well, but I cannot forgive him the stream of treacle which the orchestra was allowed to pour down our backs as the curtain fell.

*September* 24.

# "The Swallow"

## A Play by VIOLA TREE

### Everyman Theatre

WHY is it that on the stage heroines with souls to express are invariably void of any quality of interest beyond their soulfulness? Was Mary Elwes witty, companionable, or even a " good sort " ? No. Did she moon about that cottage on the links at Sunningdale, being intentionally rude to her husband's guests ? Yes. Was she just unbearable, and would not a sound smacking have been the best medicine for obstinate self-pity ? Again, yes !

If Miss Tree did not arouse interest in Mary she failed in good company. Balzac's Madame de Mortsauf, enlisting with equal ardour under the banner of the *femme incomprise*, is the most colossal bore ever achieved by genius. And Mary, be it said, is a good second. The theme of the sensitive wife tied to a husband lacking in the sensibilities is, of course, not a new one. Mortsauf was wrapped up in his illnesses, Bovary in his pigs or something of the sort, Joseph Elwes insisted upon his two rounds of golf a day. Mary's soul was all for music, and apparently the Queen's Hall was not to be reached from Sunningdale. Nor did Mary make any effort to get her own friends around her. She just moped, and you knew her for a " lone lorn creetur," likely to cry if the fire smoked. And the aggravating thing about Mary's " old 'un " was that he remained healthily and aggressively alive, and couldn't be decently mourned while his widow was making ready to marry the Italian musico, who strummed on the organ, and made sneering remarks about English manners.

But I will not press the Gummidgian simile too far. Hundreds of plays have been written round Mary in the past, and will be written round her in the future, nine-tenths of them being reducible to a formula which runs something as follows :—Act I.—Sensitive suburban wife abandons oaf-like husband in favour of romantic lover. Act II.—Sensitive runaway wife, finding she is one mistress among many, completes her disillusion just as : Act III.—Less oaf-like husband, full of reproaches, arrives and pitches into Italian lake young Bayard full of fear. Act IV.—Not at all oaf-like husband opens magnanimous arms to sensitive wounded dove. And a very good play it makes, too, whenever Sir Arthur Pinero or Mr. Sutro takes it in hand—a play full of telephones, railway-guides, family friends with watching briefs, native waiters and porters babbling " *Muchacho obligado* " and other heathenish phrases on being tipped or told to look after the luggage. Now and again one of the amusing fraternity—say M. Bernstein—will give a happy twist to the old story and

169

show Mr. Caudle emptying the vials of forgiveness on
the head of the homing Mrs. Caudle, fast asleep at his
knees.

But Miss Tree in her capacity of intellectual playwright scorns the titillations of cis- and trans-alpine
flight and pursuit.   Her characters move in a world
where the Spirit of Italy replaces Bradshaw.   Mary
runs off with the young organist, who spends the second
act trying to explain to us the Fascist movement and to
the lady the polygamous nature of man.   But surely all
the world knows that while two all-absorbing passions
cannot, by definition, exist in one man's breast at the
same time, two emotions raised to high and differing
powers can do so with convenience to their entertainer
and inconvenience to everybody else.   What happens
when their host is a woman ?   There is a play to be
written about the honourable wife who has outgrown
whatever inclination induced her to marry her simple-
ton, and yet cannot bring herself simply to walk out of
the decent fellow's house.   Miss Tree does not tackle
this any more than she tackles the purely material
factors in her situation.   Would Mary have gone
away without knowing whether her lover could foot
their bills for lodgings, food, clothes, etc., now and in
the future ?   His death leaves her penniless, but how
far does *that* determine her return ?   Suppose Mary
had had a child by husband or lover ?   Miss Tree
shirks all these awful difficulties.   Her dove just
returns to roost in a not particularly repentant mood,
and we feel that in another week she will be as rude as

ever to her husband's fellow-golfers. In fact, we are just where we were at the beginning, and I, personally, have the feeling that oafs with low handicaps are better to live with than *énervées* with exalted soul-states.

Miss Hilda Moore played the little goose for a great deal more than she was worth. Her performance was a first-class exposition of eighteen—no, twenty-two—carat martyrdom, and her last-act veils and draperies had all the sentimental appeal of one of Bouguereau's disconsolate canvases. Mr. Tristan Rawson made his gander into a fowl of some nobility. Mr. Leslie Banks's Simon Dianti was as repulsive a fellow as ever ground organ, Mr. Basil Loder got as much out of six words as some actors do out of Hamlet, and Mr. A. Scott-Gatty's shirt-front indicated that at Sunningdale three diamond studs are the correct wear with a dinner-jacket. Mesdames Margaret Yarde, Audrey Carten and Margaret Carter filled in agreeably, and Mr. Eric Lugg contributed a notable piece of acting in a small part. The enthusiasm was moderate, though there were plenty of volunteers for the pumps.

*May* 6.

# " Overture "

## A FANTASY BY SUTTON VANE

### EVERYMAN THEATRE

IS it not Samuel Butler who imagines the embryo saying to itself : Birth is terrible ? The sentimentalist, thinking on this matter, would add the word " adventure," thus giving the phrase, and with it the idea, a romantic twist. Thus—Birth is a terrible adventure. Sir James Barrie, we remember, insisted upon this nuance in the opposite connection : To die, etc., etc. Mr. Sutton Vane's *Overture* is like a lot of things. It might be a play by Butler put together in some mood of mingled pessimism and indigestion. Or *Peter Pan* re-written by Schopenhauer. Or even a pastiche of Mr. Vane by some perfervid admirer of *Outward Bound*. But, whatever it is, *Overture* remains, with certain reservations, a good play.

I will deal with the reservations first. Every story has its postulates. Let it be granted that the unborn are given the choice of making the earthward voyage or not. Let it be granted that, wearing the clothes proper to their ultimate ambition, they should have accurate foreknowledge of what that ambition is to be.

But why make it entirely unworthy ? Why endow these electors with all the human frailties fully developed and no compensating hint of divine glory, so that they embark for these shores without even the tiniest Wordsworthian rag to cover a more than Meredithian egotism ? The judge desires pomposity, the Harridan social success, the Lovers seek the selfishness of deliberate bliss. This may not be Original Sin, but it is uncommonly like Presumptive Folly. Surely, it is unduly pessimistic of Mr. Vane to suggest that it is Hell which lies about us in our infancy, that the vision splendid is a myth, and that all life grows from the beginning in the shade of the prison-house. The pathos of maturity is that the happiness which comes unsought to the child eludes the grown seeker. Mr. Vane's chickens ensue happiness—to muted murmurings in the orchestra of a certain topical tune—before they are out of the egg, and there are too many in the brood who are mean of heart.

What, presumably, we are asked to decide is whether a man would desire life if he knew that it would end in a judgeship, or a woman if she knew that she would end as a social success. Normal onerousness to be shouldered and normal ennui to be endured are the test, and not : Would it have been better for Judge Jeffreys and for Jezebel that they had never been born ? Mr. Justice Plush is careless about his charge to the jury, and Mrs. Bagleigh tipples. I do not believe that they represent their class. The lovers are in a trifle better case. She takes Him, knowing that He is an embezzler and a drunkard and married to a virago, and She is typical because good women before her have given of their comfort and not lost their goodness. The Cockney couple are admirable and may stand for their class. The Curate and the Spinster are true to life in their respective simplenesses, but we rather feel that the idyll turns out tragically because Melancholy has marked Mr. Vane for her own. In the end, the author has the rather tame conclusion that Life is hard to give up " even if the goods are not up to sample," and that the best way out of a bad job is the way of kindness. From the immensities to Ella Wheeler Wilcox is something of a decline, and if there must be pessimism, I, personally, prefer Mr. Hardy's bracing, fortitudinous sort to the despondent jelly which Mr. Vane has taken for his model at the end. To sum up : The essential thesis of this play is not stated sufficiently clearly. Throughout the audience is conscious of a jumbled interrogatory : " Is life with all its joys and sorrows worth while ? " and " Do individual wretches get sufficient out of a craven existence to make it good enough ? " Neither case gets adequate treatment, and we feel that the author has rushed his idea and butchered an overwhelming theme to make intellectual holiday.

But away with reservations ! After all, it is better to have a little play round a big idea than a big play round no idea at all, which is your West End way. The theme of *Overture* is wasted, perhaps, only in the sense in which it would have been a pity if the idea of *Othello* had occurred to Tennyson instead of to Shakespeare. Consider the play not as consecutive argument but as a series of dramas in vignette, and it is wholly admirable. The definition, in the photographer's sense, is excellent, and there is a tautness about the dialogue which is beyond praise. This writer has the enviable quality of being witty about serious matters. There is here and there a hint of steel about the directness of his ideas, and wit ripples continuously along the blade which is to drive the point home. Intending visitors should not let any question of the play's total gesture stand in their way. Taken scene by scene it is very good indeed.

Miss Nancy Price gives a magnificent picture of the Harridan who clamours for the bread of happiness and finds that it has turned into a string of emeralds. She acts throughout with a malignant intensity of greed and sense of the emptiness of satisfaction which are harrowing to watch. She is a mistress of pose, and her attitudes suggest a Medusa horrified before her glass. Miss Diana Hamilton's playing is of a quality which baffles me entirely. At times I cannot help feeling that she is an actress of minimum accomplishment. She will sit quite still, apparently thinking of nothing at all, and then, suddenly, I am aware that she has filled me with intense emotion. She has withdrawn into herself, as it were, and into a world of which the others on the stage are unaware, and she has taken me with her. I feel perfectly certain that this actress could not utter a commonplace with an air, but I know also that she has only to contemplate the tremendous, and it is as though the commonplace has gone out of the world. She is invaluable in this piece.     Mr. Allan Jeayes plays the Judge with excellent competence, and Miss Cicely Oates and Mr. Gordon Harker give admirable account of the Cockneys.    A young actor whom I cannot identify achieves horror in a thumbnail sketch of a boy-murderer, and Miss Clare Harris as the old maid presents a picture of " antiquated virginity " to move the heart of Charles Lamb.

*April* 11.

# "The Torch Bearers"

## A COMEDY BY GEORGE KELLY

### AMBASSADORS THEATRE

LET it not be thought that I am opposed to
amateur theatricals. I am not. So long as
I am not forced to make part of the audience, all is
well. Amateur shows are unbearable to behold and
adorable to take part in. The piece, for choice, should
be eighteenth century, so that one may play about with
white wigs and diamond buckles, snuff-boxes, quizzing
glasses, clouded canes, satins and laces. And then
the smell of grease-paint ! Heaven, for the amateur
actor, will have to look and smell uncommonly like a
dressing-room, or it will not be heaven.

I have some experience in the actor's art. At fourteen I was an excellent Shylock, and at fifteen an
altogether admirable Cardinal Wolsey. At least, that
was the opinion of the forty-eight fathers and forty-
eight mothers who attended the school conversazione.
At sixteen I appeared, with quite immoderate success,
in the big scene from Corneille's *Le Cid*. In French,
mark you. Leaving school, I played the lead in a
piece by Sydney Grundy, the facetiousness whereof

scaled the topmost peaks of horror. *The Snowball* I
think it was called. My last appearance was in a play
by a young amateur, entitled *The After Years*. Even
now I go hot all over when I remember that this was
about the love of a Cavalier for a Puritan maid, and, in
my opinion at the time, vastly superior to any tale of
Montague and Capulet. The piece was produced at
an evening entertainment, got up on behalf of a Girls'
Friendly Society in a remote village somewhere near
Wigan, in Lancashire. The cast was a small one,
and at the dress rehearsal the vicar threatened to veto
the play. It was improper, he said, for man and maid
to keep tryst in an empty house at midnight. Knowing that the number of available actors was small, the
author had sent all the other members of the household
to the battle of Marston Moor. For a while dismay
was rampant ; there was no time to write a chaperone's
part or to order a fresh costume. However, the vicar's
wife came to the rescue. She would borrow her great-
grandmother's shawl, enter with a teapot, and say
" Here's the tea, honey. Good-evening, my lord. I
shall be within call, miss, if you want me." Never
shall I forget the long drives in antiquated broughams
drawn by real horses over real snow thick on those real
Lancashire moors, the long rehearsals, the unending
suppers and talk. I remember to this day the pathetic
little man from the costumier's shop in Manchester,
who made us up and prattled alternately of a sick wife
and the glory of the actor's art. He suffered from
asthma, and read Henry James in secret. I remember

178

how well the play went, how ecstatic the audience was, and how friendly were the girls. For nearly a year afterwards life was entirely drab. . . .

Amateur theatricals in this country were, of course, burlesqued—that is if they can be burlesqued—once and for all in *A Pantomime Rehearsal*. Actually this was a piece of realism which Zola might have envied. *The Torch Bearers* by Mr. George Kelly, is a satire upon the Little Theatre Movement in America. Now one of the most curious things about that quaintest of countries is that " up-lift " goes hand in hand with a sentimentality which would make a rhinoceros vomit. In England we have no counterpart to the Mrs. Pampinelli of this play, though we have only to imagine a Mrs. Ormiston Chant devoted to the cause of æsthetics in the place of temperance.

I am not going to describe this play in detail. Sufficient if I say that it gives a magnificently faithful picture of the enormous gap between the amateur's aspirations and his achievements. Reach in this case exceeds grasp by an amount which is to be measured only in terms of the ludicrous. The piece is extraordinarily funny. In the first act you see Mrs. Pampinelli at rehearsal in a drawing-room, insisting upon shades so fine that a Duse could hardly grapple with them. The amateurs get through their parts well enough, and the property-man brings off his effects to time. The second act shows the back of the scenes during the actual performance of the play. Here not only do all the fine shades go by the board, but the piece itself suffers shipwreck at every turn. Entries are missed, cues are lost, properties are mislaid, moustaches come in two, the players trip up before they get on to the stage and dry up when they are on it, the curtain won't work—every kind of fiasco occurs. We do not see these things happening ; they are reflected in the perturbations of Mrs. Pampinelli directing behind the scenes, in the woes of the property man, the distress of the prompter, the agonies of the players left high and dry on the scene without a word. In the third act we are again in the drawing-room. Mrs. Pampinelli has recovered her *sang-froid*, and congratulates the company on the brilliant way in which they have upheld the banner of art. Miss Marie Tempest's company fooled it to the top of their bent, particularly Miss Athene Seyler, who clucked and fluttered about the stage like the most adorable of demented guinea-fowls. And when she was serious she sat up and begged like a French poodle. What an artist ! Mr. Ivo Dawson played the owl with portentous gravity, and Mr. Frank Allanby as Spindler was topping. Miss Tempest herself gave an admirable presentation of the higher lunacy—bland, luminous, and magnificently assured. Let me implore her to end the play with that abortive " curtain " which frustrates Mrs. Pampinelli's stage-reception. Everybody else has had his call, and the " art-directress " would take hers. But the curtain—which is, of course, inside our curtain—goes up exactly a yard and comes down again with a thud. The rope has broken. This is a magnificent effect, and the wretch's discomfiture can know no greater climax. With the third act eliminated and a one-act play substituted the venture should run to the autumn. The cream of it is excellent : the rest should be thrown away.

*April* 20.

# "Camilla States Her Case"

## A Play by GEORGE EGERTON

### Globe Theatre

NOT 'arf she don't !   And at enormous length. Camilla's part must be as long as Hamlet with a Chancellor of the Exchequer's Budget Speech thrown in.   As I came out I heard a lady say : " It isn't fair to Bunny.   Sarah herself could have done nothing with it."   I endorse this.

To the category of the *All Along* drama, I think I must now add the *Give Away* school.   By this I mean those plays which are given away the moment the curtain goes up because the case to be argued is too strong. There is an admirable comedy in the theme of the *déclassée* who is rehabilitated, and finds rehabilitation unbearably dull.   Sir Arthur Pinero hit upon this comedy, and turned it into a tragedy.   Camilla is not a *déclassée* in the accepted sense, but she is undisguisedly a film-star.   Or ought to be.   By all means take a vulgar little soul from what Hollywood calls "the floor," and let her tread the polished oak of immemorial mansions. Then let us see how long she will be able to "stick" it. And let her be vulgar of speech, or even of mind, and showy of habit, so that the baronet who has married her may have a case for irksomeness. Then let the star's side of it be put—that such as she is, she is—a woman who has fought for her independence and will not yield up what has been dearly won. Let us see the encounter between the hard-working "bunch," her friends who turn the camera-handles, and the dowager-duchesses throwing frills. And let there be some remnant of affection between husband and wife to put up a fight against those Californian odds. It would be a heartsome evening.

But Camilla was not that sort. She was perfectly well bred, perfectly well behaved, beautifully spoken, as pretty as paint, and just the sort of darling who, arriving in a country parish on Tuesday, would be installed as Lady Bountiful on Wednesday. She hadn't a thought that wasn't a wholesome one, an impulse that didn't tend towards good, never harboured a notion she couldn't have gossiped about to a parcel of children. The Elleans of the neighbourhood would have hung round her neck in clusters, the Mrs. Cortelyons would have called in droves. There was no play here because there was no contest. The baronet who married Camilla was just an imbecile who wanted to dismiss Camilla's male secretary because "the neighbourhood might talk." Whereupon Camilla had an enormous speech about spending nights with masculine stars in Alaskan shacks, Australian bush, and Patagonian pampas, and preserving the innocence of Joan of Arc among her soldiery. Who's a-denigin of it ? In the end Camilla stayed at some hotel with a lady who was also a male impersonator, and so obtained her divorce. Which was very sensible of her, but did not amount to a play.

Now a piece may be bad psychology and yet make a rattling good entertainment. This play is dull, even on low levels. It contains too much second-hand Pinero. The Baronet was Aubrey Tanqueray and Filmer Jesson rolled into one. (He actually talked about putting his house in order.) There was a confidential friend, a doctor who mooned about the Baronet's estate, throwing in an occasional oracular word *à la* Hillary. Mrs. Cortelyon and Geraldine Ridgeley were there, too, and Camilla was Paula-Nina without the temper of either. Her tirade at the end had none of the attributes of a tirade except the length, and one longed for the explosive force of " I go to no park to-morrow ! " or that tremendous exit : " We'll see ! We'll see ! " There was a dissertation upon the income-tax which must have been heard to be disbelieved. Fortunately, I have some smattering of the ways of Buddhists, and so could withdraw into meditative realms beyond the collector's reach. It should be mentioned that three times in this play did couples impart to each other at length matters of which both were perfectly aware.

I shall say nothing about Camilla. No art of actress, living or dead, could have survived this part. That of

Miss Bannerman succumbed with all that grace, charm, and elegance of which she is so perfectly the mistress. Mr. C. M. Lowne was very good as the clodhopping Baronet, and Miss Mary Rorke was a grateful presence.

*January* 7.

# " Lullaby "

## A Play by EDWARD KNOBLOCK

### Globe Theatre

MADELON was more sinned against than sinning. The poor girl wanted to keep straight on ; it was the road which insisted on taking the wrong turning. Madelon's young man would have married her had it not been for a wicked step-mother, whose temper was never agreeable and got worse when, in her step-daughter's phrase, " she presented her husband with a son of her own." Yes, Madelon talked like that.

Madelon then migrated to Paris, where she had her baby, to keep which she sewed shirts for as long as sixty hours at a stretch. As everybody in this play is in the habit of saying, " Let me see, we are in 1859, are we not ? " I may usefully note here that we have now arrived at 1875, and that Murger's *Scènes de la Vie de Bohème* had been written thirty years earlier. But there was nothing of Mimi about Madelon. She could be nobody's light o' love since her affection for her child's father still burned with a steady flame. But the news of the young man's marriage coinciding with the

186

protestations of a handsome American painter, what would you ?   And so we found the young woman installed in the Forest of Barbizon.   Here it seemed that Madelon's wandering barque had come to anchor, since her love for the American painter was obviously an ever-fixed mark to look on tempests and be never shaken.   But a heavy American father's apoplectic seizure transcends your ordinary storm ;  it is a typhoon. Therefore the young man had to go back to America, and the young woman starved virtuously until, for the child's sake, she took to her bosom a bogus Italian count.

We have now arrived at 1881, and the scene in Madelon's boudoir and in the Restaurant Pompadour fills the eyes with reminiscent delight.   Madelon herself wears the gowns which in the 'eighties Sarah Bernhardt wore as the Lady of the Camellias.   There hangs over the piece here a faint fragrance of patchouli, quickly dispelled, however, by the appearance of handsome Miss Violet Farebrother in dresses reminiscent of Mrs. Kendal in *The Ironmaster*.   Twenty years now pass, and we arrive at the City Wall, Tunis, and also at the play's third and best manner.   We have had Murger and Dumas *fils*, with an interpolation borrowed straight from Miss Constance Collier's part in *Our Betters*, and here at last is Maupassant.   The story of the courtesan who will not talk with sailors because she has learned that her long-abandoned child is in the navy is exactly the kind of thing which might have appeared in the *Gil Blas* over the signature " Maufrigneuse."   This scene is well observed, and

187

exceedingly well acted by Miss Margaret Bannerman. Then Madelon had a scuffle with a sailor whose revolver went off. So Madelon went off too, and did twenty years in prison. And we see her at ninety years of age advising a young woman not to go to a night club.

This is exactly the sort of play to which Mrs. Markham might have taken her two boys and even little Mary. One can imagine the conversation at breakfast next day. "Tell me, dear Mamma," Richard would ask, "was Madelon really wicked?" "I should rather say, my dear, that she was the victim of circumstances." "And pray, Mamma," little Mary would catechise, "what does that mean exactly?" "It means, my love, that it is time for me to resume telling you about dear Hengist and Horsa." The truth about this piece is that it is not more true to life than the patrons at the cinema demand. Mr. Knoblock is an incorrigible sentimentalist. He cannot bear to think that the Madelons of this world are what they are except by conspiracy of fate.

That the piece is ultimately intended for the film is shown by the absence of care in the writing. This is at once stilted and common-place. "Money will always be money to us French peasants—every sou is a drop of blood" is just *not* what a French peasant will say. Nor do Italian counts, bogus or otherwise, preface their remarks by saying, "I am afraid we of the old Italian nobility . . .," though Mr. Scott-Gatty almost made us think that they might. In fact, I am afraid

188

that the whole piece, with the exception of the one short scene in Tunis, is banality itself, though a film audience would probably like it for the fact that it tells a story straight-forwardly without any kind of æsthetic implication. Apart from the principal *rôle* there was not much scope for the actors, though one would single out Miss Violet Farebrother and Mr. Herbert Grimwood for good performances.

What of Madelon ? Well, the part is obviously both arduous and snippety. Miss Bannerman had an exhausting task, and brought very considerable skill to what one thought to be a collection of thumbnail sketches rather than full portraits. That she can play the charming young girl of fifteen adorably we all know, and that she could play an old woman of ninety well enough—given the time to settle down to it—we now firmly believe. I thought the whole of the " Marguerite Gautier " scene in the third act was delicious. The evening was a great personal triumph for this most accomplished actress. How clever of her to efface seventy years in as many seconds, and appear finally as the charming lady to whom we are all devoted !

*November* 6.

# " Lavender Ladies "

## A Comedy by DAISY FISHER

### Comedy Theatre

HERE is a piece which wanted throwing back into the past. Only this time the gap should have been one of at least seventy years. The Lavender Ladies really come out of *Cranford*, and if we want to date the play exactly we must suppose them to have lingered on from the age of Mrs. Gaskell to that of Sarah Grand. Are there still any popular novelists advocating Free Love? And are there any young girls ready to be taken in by them? Doubtless romances are now being woven round night clubs, but it is to be supposed that the modern young woman knows all there is to be known about those resorts, and that she would tell the romancer that of love, free or otherwise, there is no question. I am not convinced about the young girl in this play who, deeply loving one man and desiring to bear children to him and to nobody else, deems marriage an ignoble and degrading ceremony. The woe produced by a purely ninetyish, emancipatory obstinacy cuts no ice to-day. As for the

Lavender Ladies—I take it that they, too, have long been laid in their graves. Virginity, dragonsome as that of Miss Anne, faded and album-pressed as that of Miss Rose, is no longer the wear.

"Nay, mamma, if he is not to be animated by Cowper ! " said Marianne Dashwood, discussing her sister Eleanor's young man. Nay, dear reader, if you are not to be animated by Mrs. Gaskell ! is probably the kindest criticism of Miss Fisher's play. Where it is funny, it is very funny ; where it is goody-goody, it is tedious. The piece is well written throughout in the way of nicely-devised dialogue. Expectations are pleasantly aroused and neatly satisfied, but the felicity is on small scale. The first and third acts are delightful in their recapitulation of outrageous propriety. There sits Miss Anne, with a back stiff as Miss Murdstone's, bullying her sister and getting ready to put on a semblance of humanity as the hour of eleven approaches. There sits Miss Rose, the timorous sister, whose heart Miss Anne insists was broken long ago and who plucks up courage, also towards eleven o'clock, to declare that nothing of the sort ever happened to it. Then there is Miss Tabitha Harrow, the old Scottish housekeeper, who takes her orders with some simulation of obedience and carries them out as she thinks fit. All this is very deftly and charmingly done. It was about ten o'clock before we heard the sound of a not unwelcome masculine voice. There were only two men, counting a boy as nothing, in the play ; and their scenes went some way to prove that if Miss Fisher has a good deal of Mrs. Gaskell's strength, she has also some of Jane Austen's weakness.

If this play runs—which I think it undoubtedly will —it will be owing first to its " pleasant taste " which some of us are churlish enough to confuse with insipidity, and, second, to the admirable way in which it is acted. Sometimes I wonder that players do not massacre authors who insist upon writing parts alleged to suit their individualities, and theatre managers who pretend that they can play nothing else. Take the Lavender Ladies, for example, played of course to perfection by Miss Louise Hampton and Miss Mary Jerrold. Let me confess that my heart sometimes sinks a little when I see on my programme the names of these so admirable artists. The confession is at no cost of gallantry, my compunction being for the artists. I know that each will repeat a performance which by now has become second nature to her. Nature is perfect, and so, too, is second nature ; but it must be dreadfully boring for an actress to sail none but seas which she herself has charted *ad nauseam.* How would it be if, say on two evenings a week, these ladies were to exchange parts ? A first-class actor can play Iago as well as Othello, and it is a slight to Miss Hampton to suggest that she can portray nothing but vinegar, and to Miss Jerrold that she knows no quality but sugar. Miss Jean Cadell was allowed a Scotch accent, otherwise the character was largely as before. Given Mr. Herbert Marshall's words, I think I could have foretold every accent, inflection, intonation, and gesture. All were admirable, but is Mr. Marshall never to be allowed to be admirable in some other way ?

Possibly the most interesting performance was that of Miss Elissa Landi as the ingenuous heroine. Miss Landi, who, by singular misfortune, has never been cast for anything except leading parts, showed for the first time that she may, with great study and diligence, ultimately become something more than a talented amateur. She has intelligence and a certain power of natural emotion. This is not as yet well regulated, and her movements at present are not under control. The long and short of it is that this young actress has an arduous apprenticeship before her. Patient practice in the provinces and *rôles* like Celia and Nerissa would do her immense good, and she could then come back to the London stage equipped for parts which are at present beyond her. But I repeat that her performance in this play is the most promising I have seen.

*July* 29.

# " Cristilinda "

## A Comedy by MONCKTON HOFFE

### Garrick Theatre

WE are always being told that the proper way to criticise a work of art is to measure achievement against intention, that is, first to decide what the author set out to do, and then declare how far he has succeeded. What, exactly, was in Mr. Monckton Hoffe's mind when he sat down to write *Cristilinda*? The piece as performed is a light comedy, in Lady Bracknell's words, " of more than usually revolting sentimentality." Yet one would not willingly imagine that this was how Mr. Hoffe conceived it.

The play has an enormously long introduction of quite unusual merit. The scene is the single music-hall of some one-horse manufacturing town. The occasion is the unveiling of an old master—Fra Filippo Lippi's St. Etheldreda—presented to the church of that name by the ennobled brewer who rules the surrounding roost. On the stage are assembled all the bigwigs proper to such an occasion—the bashful, competent, minor Royalty, the Bishop, mellifluous and many-sided, St. Etheldreda's priest, white-haired and humble, the fussy, talkative Mayor, the local, loud-voiced Labour Member, the Magnate himself prodigal of tips direct from the mouths of his racehorses, the *pukka* Marquis in whose veins runs the blood of Tudor stupidity. All these characters are admirably observed, and reproduced with Galsworthian fidelity. The objection is not valid, I think, which claims that all the author had to do here was to attend a public meeting and take short-hand notes. Let any such objector make the attempt, and see whether the result remotely approaches reality. This introduction was full of quiet delight, and for the best part of an hour the audience beamed and chuckled. Alas, that the body of the play so deftly introduced should turn out to be a farrago of hopeless nonsense !

I imagine that the doltish, clowning humanity which clod-hopped through this piece was conceived in fairy-land. I imagine Mr. Hoffe saw in Cristilinda an elfish little person for whose eyes had been scooped " the wood-brown pools of Paradise," in her lover a young painter straight from the pages of Henri Murger, in her father a circus proprietor steeped in the traditions of the ring like Goncourt's Brothers Zemganno. I imagine that he placed these ideal personages in a setting like a canvas by Tolouse Lautrec. Paint these simple creatures, and I imagine that you could invest them with singular charm. Why, therefore, not a charming stage-play ? Does the young artist's father object to his son's alliance with a circus-rider ? Very well then, the girl herself shall break off the engage-ment, mobilising to that end whole cohorts of immolatory tarradiddles as to her being somebody else's mistress. The scene, you say, will be the third act of *La Dame aux Camélias* all over again. But old Duval was always a good card to play, and, anyhow, the innocent Cristilinda should be good for as many tears as the guilty Marguerite. Charming fancy, again, to show the gradual decline of the circus, the decadence *à la* César Birotteau of the old ring-master, who shall, however, gather up sufficient strength to deliver a pæan to tradition on the lines of Coquelin's famous tirade in *La Montansier*. A capital idea, doubtless, to see the little circus-lady crippled owing to a stumble on the part of that parcel of splints and spavins, her horse, and though a cripple and twenty years older still her father's prop and stay. There was ingenuity in the idea. Cristilinda's picture, painted by the boy-artist and sold for twelve pounds, might well, by passing into the hands of fakers, become the Lippo Lippi of the presentation scene. There was pathos here, for the little lady would find compensation for her broken heart and limb in the thought of the balm brought by her image to the hearts of humble worshippers.

That, one thinks, is probably something of what Mr. Hoffe imagined. Put on the stage his play did whatever may be the opposite of melting into thin air. Instead of the queer little child of nature—for whom the model was already to be found in Hauptman's Hannele —we had the glorious womanhood and peony-like radiance of Miss Isobel Elsom. Miss Elsom is one of our most sophisticated actresses who knows every trick of the trade, and lets you know that she knows it ; but the quaint fancy of a child is one thing, and the imbecility of a mature character is another.  Miss Elsom did her very best with the part, but what is the use of any actress trying to be unutterably childish when every ounce of her being conveys a picture of the finest flush of womanhood as Sir Frederick Leighton might have painted it ?  Then there was the circus-master of Mr. Allan Aynesworth.  One knows that even in the height of his grandeur a " General " Christopherson is something dingy in habit, and that the vernacular creeps into his talk.  " Very good," said Tchehov to the actor who first played Trigorin, " but you want check trousers and shabby boots."  Mr. Hoffe ought to have said something of the kind to Mr. Aynesworth, who seemed as though he could hardly bear to lower himself to the arrant vulgarian.  The actor wore the glossiest of hats and spoke in his glossiest accent, his French was beyond reproach, and his air, as he stood in the dead middle of the stage, was of one who would not be afraid to bandy compliments with his Sovereign. There was not the faintest suspicion that the old man's table-manners were anything but irreproachable, and one thought with regret of old Snazelle, who put his knife in his mouth, saying with gusto, " Manners is my strong point.  See what I mean ? "  As Miss Elsom spoke the purest Girtonese, the first of their many colloquies brought the play toppling about our ears.

Once out of fairyland the disaster was complete. One listened in amazement while a full-grown young woman babbled such fantasies as " A husband is a woman's little child until another comes to take his place."  Let me exempt from carping criticism Mr. Frank Freeman, whose artist-lover seemed to me to be a singularly perfect performance in exactly the right key.  It would be very interesting to discover how this piece would play with Cristilinda acted by some child-actress of genius, say Miss Angela Baddeley, and the circus-master given by an actor with a sense of buffoonery who did not remind one of the late Mr. Gladstone perorating under one of Hawarden's oaks. In these conditions it might be worthy of Mr. Norman O'Neill's delightful incidental music.

*October* 21.

# " The Sea Urchin "

## A Comedy by J. Hastings Turner

### Strand Theatre

# " Tarnish "

## A Play by Gilbert Emery

### Vaudeville Theatre

TWO well-thumbed novelettes. But *The Sea Urchin* is wrongly named. Better to have called it *Peggyanna*, since it is obviously compounded of *Peg o' My Heart* and *Pollyanna*. The charge of plagiarism does not lie ; Mr. Turner has simply taken pick and shovel and gone to work in the same mine of toothsome rock whence those sickly masterpieces were produced. Add, too, the fact that the heroine has some small dash of *Anna Christie*. Blench not, reader, at the serious possibilities here. We are given to understand from certain of the heroine's leers and byplay that from the age of seven—is it ?—she has hobnobbed with all that New York underworld with which Mr. Eugene O'Neill's waif made us so pathetically familiar. But she is tarnished, if I may borrow Mr. Emery's word only intellectually. Or, to use Miss Glaspell's idiom, you might say that she is affected only in so far as " awareness " is concerned. Spiritually, Fay's life has been passed among fields of asphodel.

So innocent in her Joan-ness was this maid that she could travel in a French barque—or was it a ketch ? —the sole feminine companion of six rude French sailors, who deviated no whit from the polite traditions of their race. Fay was bound for Ireland, where, or so she was informed, there were no police and she could give scope to her free and careless nature, her boundings and skippings, and the untrammelled warbling of her native wood-notes wild. But the barque was wrecked on the inhospitable coast of Cornwall, and the poor innocent was carried into the worst graces and back bedroom of—would you believe it ?—her inhospitable aunts. It is only in sentimental comedy that these million-to-one chances come off. Antecedent to the shipwreck the Misses Wynchbeck had told us that but for them and a scapegrace brother long swallowed up by the trail of the Yukon the Wynchbeck family was extinct. And lo ! this bit of human flotsam thrown up by the wave turned out to be their long-lost niece.

And, of course, the elder Miss Wynchbeck was inhospitable and forbidding only after Betsey Trotwood's manner ; her frownings and scoldings concealed a heart. She did, finally, consent to the brandy being brought. Conceivable, too, that if the piece had contained anybody possessed of Mr. Dick's awful sanity, Miss Mary might have taken those remedial measures ordained in Copperfield's case and given poor Fay a bath. But that, it might be argued, would have been a work of supererogation. Too much of water hadst thou, poor Ophelia—I mean Fay. Miss Minnie, the younger aunt, was a poor thing who spent her life cherishing a broken heart. Who had broken it ? Who but the father of Fay's lover, Sir Trevor Trebarrow, a Cornish knight given to hunting something or other in a cloth cap. But there being a feud between the Wynchbecks and the Trebarrows, the rest of the play ran along the familiar Montague-Capulet lines.

Another title might have been *Peggyana*. For Fay being played by Miss Peggy O'Neil, the piece is really no more than a vehicle for a display of Miss Peggy's Peggyishness. I have no doubt that this most popular actress sends the minds of her admirers questing after strange images of beauty. Some will see Joan—less of Arc than of Kansas City—others may behold a Mliss. But whatever the comparison, there can be no doubt that hearts were never laid waste by a more devastating winsomeness. Winsomeness which rose above the play like the Great Wheel at Blackpool, visible on a clear day from Southport across the estuary of Ribble. Winsomeness with power to dissolve the bricks and mortar of the Strand Theatre and pierce to the street outside. But, personally, I should have been less distressed if the artist had not fallen so willing a victim to the trick of the child-impersonator who cannot keep finger out of mouth and eye. Miss Helen Haye is a distinguished actress who has chosen, for inscrutable reasons, to adorn this piece ; and in the depiction of invertebracy none could have excelled Miss Margaret Watson. Messrs. Clifford Heatherley and Mr. Arthur Pusey gave of their best.

*Tarnish* is a novelette for a more advanced reader. Here, again, coincidence is up to her old tricks. When young Emmett Carr decides to marry Joan Tevis he rightly decides to be no more a visitor at the flat of that light-o'-love, Nettie Dark. And when Joan's father, a disgraceful old fribble, returns from the bank with his six-monthly pension, whom should he encounter but Nettie ! She relieves him of his wallet. So Joan determines to visit the girl and get the money back— since the family is left without a cent. And, of course, it must happen that on that very evening Nettie lures young Emmett back to the flat for a farewell, and one more glass of the Duchess of Strood's Félix Poubelle, Carte d'Or (see *The Gay Lord Quex*). The *scène-à-faire* occurs when the three meet, and a very good scene it is, too.

Nettie is not a bad sort. She has dispensed one-fifth of her booty in pure charity, and the glimpses we are afforded of her character are such as to make the moralist wonder why it is that the reprehensible of this world should be allowed to be such good company. By natural or Providential law the monkey, one understands, is warned by bitterness of taste of the nature of poisonous berries. But the human monkey has been accorded no such advantage. To him that fruit is sweetest which he ought not to touch—which seems very unfair. But, moralising apart, Mr. Emery has contrived a very exciting and amusing scene, in which he has forgotten none of the familiar tear-compelling devices—the bad girl's wounded sensibility and the good girl's dismay at discovering that though her knight has no fear he is not without reproach. Faults in the piece are that the first act is too long and that there is nothing left for the third except a drawn-out scene of reconciliation. But the second act is good enough to discount these minor blemishes. Miss Olga Lindo gets every ounce out of Nettie, and Miss Nora Swinburne does not bore us with Joan. Mr. Francis Lister brings intelligence as well as charm to Emmett Carr, and the trio pull off the big scene with as much aplomb as if they had been doing it for forty years. If acting could have turned a feuilleton into *belles lettres* these three would have done it.

*March* 30, 31.

# " Anyhouse "

## A Play by F. TENNYSON JESSE

### Ambassador's Theatre

IT is extraordinary how popular Ibsen is whenever
he is played under another name. *Anyhouse* set
me first thinking how little out-of-date is the fifty-
year-old *Pillars of Society*, and then wondering whether
the audience would have accepted Ibsen's cheque on
Proper Feeling without Miss Jesse's second signature.
There is no question of plagiarism. You may say
succinctly that humbug is humbug whether it be in
London suburb or Norwegian coast town, that hypo-
crisy's stuffy air can be freshened only by the opening
of windows, and that whether the windows look out
upon gloomy fiord or sunny High Street the gesture of
opening must be more or less the same.

Still, it awoke old memories to find all the ladies of
Mrs. Bernick's sewing-party, including their spiritual
director, summed up in the person of the egregious
Agatha Blaize. Once more we heard the complacent
intoning of Schoolmaster Rörlund. " These poor
fallen creatures for whose rescue we are working may
be compared to soldiers wounded on the field of battle ;

you, ladies, are the kind-hearted sisters of mercy who prepare the lint for these stricken ones, etc., etc." This was Agatha's vein when the charity was without her doors. But within matters looked differently. Agatha would not cast Lizzie, the erring house-parlourmaid, into the street ; but she could and did arrange for her to be taken to a home for fallen women. And we feel that Agatha will behave to Lizzie, after her baby is born, exactly as Mrs. Bernick behaved to Dina Dorf, ostentatiously forgiving and vengefully unforgetting— only with Dina it was her mother's sin—saying no word yet full of mute reproach, making the poor girl feel that she is " different," and generally turning life for her into a kind-hearted hell.

Then who but Johan Tönnesen was Agatha's brother-in-law, Torquil Blaize, Simon Blaize's cattle-ranching brother ? In the Ibsen play the stout fellow carried off Lona Hessel, the young woman who knew her own mind, to be his chum, and Dina, the lorn little sewing-maid, to be his wife. Miss Jesse entrusted to Torquil's care as farm-hand that determined wench Maidie Blaize—who expected from marriage no delights that she knew not of and jibbed at a union devised to restore her father's credit—and as spouse Jenny, the Blaizes' kitchen-maid. Who, again, but Ella Rentheim, honest with herself and with everybody else, was Aunt Julia, Simon's sister ? But I would not push the comparison too far, and make it only as a protest against the too easy assumption that Ibsen's prose works are as dead as mutton. Shall I say that

Miss Jesse's play is as fresh as the New Zealand sort ?

Every piece of writing has a total gesture, and that of *Anyhouse* is to the effect that pretenders are dead, and only non-pretenders are alive. This story of a parlour-maid and her lover, the ex-soldier who can get neither work nor dole, of the over-speculative merchant who would buy a rich son-in-law, of the daughter in wide-eyed revolt is for the greater part told perhaps even more after the manner of Miss Braddon than of Ibsen. But in the last act the ex-soldier, now engaged to wait at the Blaizes' dinner-party, turns out to be in league with a foreign revolutionary, who holds up the whole party with a revolver. The fellow is mad. He has already mortally wounded Lizzie, and now intends to shoot the worthless members of the family, making of their bodies such a bonfire as, by Communist grace, shall never be put out. He is overpowered by a lucky chance, and the company, having secured him, fall to squabbling as to which of them are desirable, useful sheep and which undesirable, useless goats.

The stage presented a curious spectacle here. On the right was the Spirit of Bolshevism bound and writhing in a chair ; to the left was the dying parlourmaid consoled by the ex-soldier. Kitchenmaid and cook were praying silently. Up-stage a fossilised grand-parent, who had babbled to no discoverable purpose of test-tubes and spontaneous generation, was being comforted by Aunt Julia. In the corners Simon and Agatha were engaged in tearing their hair as though they would pull Respectability up by the roots to see what it was made of. The dead-centre of the stage was taken by the cattle-rancher for the purpose of offering such observations as occurred to him. Somebody said something about 'phoning for the doctor and the police, and, indeed, final'y this was done. I suppose the interval had to be filled in somehow, but I simply refuse to credit that in real life it would have been filled in with small talk on Big Subjects. I do not believe that any man who has just escaped death could think of an abstract noun to save his life—even a second time. But the cattle-rancher had an itch for philosophy—did he not seriously put it to Maidie that she did not " trust Life enough " ? Here was his chance.

The trouble, of course, was that Miss Jesse tried to cram more into her play than it would hold. It was rather like being invited to gaze for two acts upon an ordinary plant out of the potting-shed at the bottom of the garden, and then being bidden to watch it grow in the third act into a whole Forest of Thought. Now Indian jugglery of this sort is beyond Miss Jesse's powers. Besides, we wanted vengeance on Jenny's— I mean, Lizzie's—case. We were interested, absorbed even, in the poor child. If the ex-soldier had merely stolen the spoons, and if Lizzie, deprived of such meagre protection as the down-and-out and imprisoned can afford, had escaped from Agatha's clutches into the Thames—why then there were a case to cry to Heaven. We wanted to know what Agatha and Simon would have had to say, to pluck out the heart of their pretentious mystery. Instead, we must speculate upon the Soul of Man. What I, personally, wondered at was the persistence of the old theory that people can only behave usefully and decently on condition that they emigrate and drive cattle about the pampas of Patagonia.

The scenery and furniture were rather aggressively expressionistic. Why should people in Balham be supposed to sit about in green chairs of cabalistic design and help themselves from a hippopotamic sideboard which no van, however plain, would consent to deliver ? Among the players I should like to praise Miss Dora Gregory as Agatha, Miss Hilda Moore as Maidie, Mr. Walter Hudd as the ex-soldier, and Mr. Ivor Barnard as the revolutionary. Mr. Tom Nesbit's steer-wrestler did not quite convince me. The best thing of the evening was undoubtedly Miss Olive Sloane's Lizzie. It is hard to tell how good this actress really may be. She has a brilliant gift of low comedy, as several parts have shown. *Low Tide* proved that she has power and explicit pathos. In this piece she conveyed an almost too piteous expression of hardly articulate woe.

*March* 12.

# Revivals

# "The Rivals"

## By RICHARD BRINSLEY SHERIDAN

### Lyric Theatre, Hammersmith

LADY GORGIUS MIDAS, we remember, went to see the acting in a French " drame," and desired that the play's meaning should escape her. The plot of *The Rivals* must escape anybody, and the continued success of this magnificent comedy proves once again that when a man of genius sets out to tell a story it really matters very little what sort of story he has to tell. Probably the best way with old plays is to take their convolutions for granted and not try to straighten them out. A, disguised as B, loves C, who adores B and must marry A, who has for rivals D and E—all this is very perplexing and of no importance. The critics of 1775 were horribly down on " poor Sherry " for the wrong reason ; let those of 1925 praise him for the right ones.

All this is but the prologue to the bald statement that the present revival is entirely worthy of the piece, the place, the one and a half centenary, and the two Mr. Playfairs—the producer and the actor. Only I should have put the actor first. For in the way of production Mr. Playfair has done little except achieve three miracles in the way of casting, of which he himself is one. And allow Mr. Norman Wilkinson's fancy perfect liberty in exquisiteness of dress and decoration. And empty the stage of all furniture save the sofa upon which Lydia must languish, and the dressing-table before which Bob Acres must make his toilet. And ensure that these pieces shall be delightful to the eye. And give us the whole text, or nearly the whole, and refrain from unnecessary embroideries, and bring his actors to the bubbling-point of his own effervescent gaiety. Apart from these things Mr. Playfair, the producer, does not call for comment. But Mr. Playfair, the actor, does. His Bob Acres is an entirely credible and rational personage, though the amount of reasoning power be limited. The actor quite rightly makes him a cut or two above Lumpkin, and has an expression of native wonder and bewilderment which befits the character admirably. There is dignity in the little fellow, who retains a pathetical shred of belief in all the fudge about " honour." To clown this part is to ensure its perfect tediousness, and this actor never bored us for a moment.

Shall I praise Miss Isabel Jeans for her Lydia ? I think not ; one doesn't praise a rose for being a rose. Perhaps there may have been Lydias more fragrant. delicious, and provocative. Perhaps other actresses have been daintier rogues in porcelain, have sailed the floor in better imitation of a skiff before a summer breeze, have given the shimmering beauty of the lines more adorable languor and steelier point. These things are a conception of the mind, and, as I think, an unlawful conception. Certain it is that Miss Jeans's recital of the projected elopement—" so amiable a ladder of ropes, conscious moon, four horses, etc., etc." —fell on the ear in cascade of lovely sound unheard since Miss Evans's " Adieu, my morning thoughts."

But the Faulkland of Mr. Claude Rains was better still. Miss Jeans could not have helped being good ; Mr. Rains easily might. The most that any actor has ever aspired to in this part has been a decent failure ; Mr. Rains made it a blazing success. He delivered the outpourings of rodomontade as they were Almanzor's purple torrents, and with every magnificence of voice and gesture. The modesty of nature being over-stepped by just that degree which secures the very nicety of burlesque, the performance made the best of both worlds—the tragic and the comic. Let me seize the occasion to say again that Mr. Rains is one of the very best actors in England, and perhaps the only one a foreigner having no English would appreciate. He has *temperament*, which is really the one thing that matters. An actor who is 90 per cent. temperament and 10 per cent. brains is a great actor ; reverse the proportions and you get a duffer.

It is a standing reproach to West End managers that Mr. Rains can only be seen when one is on pilgrimage. This actor can play nine or ten entirely different parts superbly, therefore they think he cannot be trusted to fill a middling *rôle* adequately. He is neither a stock figure nor a tailor's dummy. He does not look like your manager's pre-conceived notions of a lawyer's clerk, bishop, publican, or prize-fighter. He happens to be that, from the managerial point of view, supremely useless thing, an actor, and a very fine actor. Is he, perhaps, not six foot tall? But then " little " Robson was not a giant. Mr. Rains is not a friend of mine, and I offer this pæan out of simple duty.

What about Mrs. Malaprop? Mr. Playfair has flouted the obvious in selection, and the obvious has had its revenge. Miss Dorothy Green is an exceedingly capable actress, whose personality keeps her a hundred miles from the part. The lady's humours are broad and fat ; Miss Green's sallies can only be thin, acid, and shrewish. The malapropisms are surely a very boiling-over in gusto ; their creatrix must lick her chops and hold her sides at each conquest over uncommon talk. That Miss Green cannot do this is not her fault. Mr. Guy Lefeuvre is, perhaps, not quite in the skin of Sir Lucius, who might be a character out of Lever's novels. There is too much charm and too little Pistol in him. Mr. Douglas Burbidge's Captain is a dull dog, but then Sheridan made him so.

*March 5.*

# "Caste"

## A COMEDY BY T. W. ROBERTSON

### EVERYMAN THEATRE

THAT *Caste* is an unassailable masterpiece is proved by the fact that not even the present production at the Everyman Theatre entirely overthrew it. The setting was not good, the piece was cut to ribbons in deplorable fashion, and half the actors were pointedly and triumphantly mis-cast. Let me take these matters in their order. "Eccles! Eccles! There never was an Eccles. He don't exist," exclaimed the Marquise de St. Maur, and one would say with equal emphasis that the Little House in Stangate never existed in the way in which the producer of this revival has seen it. In the mind's eye "Be it ever so humble," is inscribed over that parlour door. The Everyman stage is admittedly small, but by some strange perversity the parlour of the Eccles family was made to take on spaciousness. Not even Esther would have had the taste in 1867 to cover her father's walls in cool distemper, while the pictures were not those with which the family would have surrounded themselves, being exactly the thing for which a modern collector ransacks Chelsea. Only the tablecloth and the gas brackets seemed to me to be real. It would not be against my argument that each piece of furniture did actually come out of the apartment of some ballet dancer in the 'sixties ; the assemblage gave one no such impression.

Will readers believe that the whole of the Marchioness's reminiscences of Froissart were omitted ? The fearsome old lady is a figure of gorgeous fun, and one to whom the later Lady Bracknell owes a great deal. The following passage, fortunately left intact, is at least as good as anything in Wilde :—

> MAR : My boy, I am sure, will never make a *mésalliance*. He is a D'Alroy, and by his mother's side *Planta-genista*. The source of our life stream is royal.
>
> GEO : How is the Marquis ?
>
> MAR : Paralysed. I left him at Spa with three physicians. He always is paralysed at this time of the year ; it is in the family. The paralysis is not personal, but hereditary.

Polly, too, was shorn of some of her best lines. Will it be believed that her first speech on the opening of the third act was cut short at " How annoyed Susan Smith will be ! " ? How all the Pollys one has ever seen used to lick their lips over : " Mrs. Samuel Gerridge presents her compliments to Miss Susan Smith, and Mrs. Samuel Gerridge requests the favour of Miss Susan Smith's company to tea, on Tuesday evening next, at Mrs. Samuel Gerridge's house " !

One remembers how they used to pause, deliver themselves of a compassionate " Poor Susan ! " and then,
squaring their elbows to the table, begin again :
" P.S.—Mrs. Samuel Gerridge―― " To take this
from Polly is to take all the heart out of the actress.
And one asked what the world was coming to when, in
that dramatic revelation at the end, Polly was found
dispensing with the piano.

Sam Gerridge was in little better case. Why should
the poor fellow not have been allowed to tell us that
" Life is a railway journey and Mankind a passenger,
first-class, second-class, third-class " ? Why might he
not warn us that " Any person found riding in a superior
class to that for which he has taken his ticket will be
removed at the first station stopped at, according to the
bye-laws of the company " ? Why should Sam not
call Polly his " brightest batswing and most brilliant
burner " ? Why should he not tell us that on thinking
of her his words glow " like red-hot solder " ? Why
deprive him of the magnificent soliloquy which begins
with the description of the Royal Arms—" a lion and a
unicorn a-standin' on their 'ind legs, doin' nothin' furiously, with a lozenge between 'em "—goes on to discover
that honourables is " mammas, not mothers," and ends
by describing Esther asleep and " that great, big, 'eavy,
'ulking, overgrown dragoon prowlin' outside, ready to
fly at 'er lips, and strangle 'er in 'is strong, lovin'
arms " ? Why rob the poor plumber of the moment
when he can lay his greasy head upon the table and
burst into tears ? There were filchings even from

Esther. I can remember to this day how, as a boy, my heart leapt at the poor girl when I first saw her come down stage and heard her declaim : " My lion and my love ! Oh ! to be a soldier, and to fight the wretches who destroyed him—who took my darling from me ! To gallop miles upon their up-turned faces ! " To this day I shall never forget how the actress suited the action to the word and dashed frantically across the stage to break down on the words " upturned faces," resting her head on the mantelpiece and raising it presently to discover Captain Hawtree's letter. What sense of the Theatre can anybody have to allow such effectiveness to go by the board ? And these were only some of the omissions.

As Captain Hawtree Mr. Leslie Banks was quite pathetically the wrong person. All that intensity of manner and ferocity of being which have stood Mr. Banks in good stead in a hundred parts are hostile to this bland and luminous masher. Hawtree should be redolent of unction, magnificent in person, imbecile and good-hearted, fatuous and droll. His collar should be of that height which prevents him from seeing the world at his feet, and his languor should amount also to physical distress. The fellow is very little removed from an idiot, which is the one class of personage with whom Mr. Banks, clever though he is, is entirely unable to cope. I shall only say of Miss Beatrix Thomson's Polly that you could easily have mistaken her for Esther. It would be difficult to conceive anything more utterly unlike the Marchioness than Miss Violet

Farebrother's impersonation. We saw before us an extremely handsome woman in the late 'thirties and the fullest flush of vigour. Mr. Aubrey Mather's Eccles was middling, and I have never seen the filling of the pipe go for so little. Miss Mercia Swinburne's Esther was pleasant. Two good performances were the George D'Alroy of Mr. Arthur Pusey and the Sam Gerridge of Mr. Victor Stanley, but of these only the former had what Henry James calls the " tone of time."

I repeat that the enormous vitality and actor-proof quality of this old comedy is proved by the fact that, in spite of the poorest performance I have ever seen, the audience were moved in the right way in as many of the right places as were left.

*August 3.*

# "On 'Change"

## A Farcical Comedy Adapted by E. LAURENCE AND H. F. MALTBY

### Savoy Theatre

ACTION and reaction are equal and opposite. Having supped the season's fill of absinthean and dopish horror, the playgoer may now, if he likes, take the milk-and-watery way to bed. Fortunately, there are other ways of enjoying oneself in the theatre besides just listening to the play. For example, during Mr. Courtneidge's revival of *On 'Change* " the mind could have cast itself into the producer's mould and revelled in a lost opportunity. What a pity the occasion was not seized to present the old farce as a collector's piece under the title of *We Antediluvians*. There is not, never was, and never can be anything modern about this forty-years-old farce. We are reminded that it was first produced in 1885. But there is nothing stubborn about facts, as Signor Pirandello is always pointing out ; and I should put the spiritual date of this piece at some ten years earlier. *On 'Change* is virtually the bridge between the late plays of Tom Robertson and the early ones of Sir Arthur

Pinero. (The original author may have been a foreigner, but he was a bridge for all that.) But, taking the date at its face value, 1885 is an admirable producer's period. In this year Mr. Henry Irving went to America, Mr. and Mrs. Bancroft bade farewell to the stage, and young Mr. Pinero made his last appearance as an actor. What a chance to produce for antiquity !

It is possible that originally the *clou* of this piece was the Scottish Professor's dabblings in stocks and shares. But in comparison with the deep-sea questing at the Aldwych Theatre of recent years the Stock Exchange waters at the Savoy run a trifle shallow. No, in this sentimental farce it is the sentiment which counts. In the 'eighties it cannot have seemed preposterous that a seedy young man who has rescued a well-bred young lady from a cab-accident should be dismissed with thanks and a ten-pound note. Those were the days when " ordinary " young men were expected to behave as such, when no employee dared raise his eyes to his employer's daughter, and any such act was fraught with the direst emotional complications. There was a time when the ultimate fate of the amorous swain and his diffident, yet coming-on, young lady might have appeared to hang in the balance, and the proper thing, I submit, to have done with this piece was to trick it out in those old habits in which such tremulous suspense was wont to be dressed.

What fun it would have been to have hit the exact note of '85 ! The 'sixties, in their absurdity, are easy enough ; and so, too, are the 'nineties. The middle 'eighties should be sufficiently ticklish to put any producer on his mettle.   In the matter of ladies' costume, the bustle was dying and the leg-of-mutton sleeve was being born.   For the men smoking caps and velvet jackets were going out of fashion, though red silk handkerchiefs were still inserted in evening waistcoats.   And then the furniture !   The æsthetic craze was only just starting, and one still moved precariously about drawing-rooms encumbered with " what-nots," " occasional " chairs, and the dear, dead, stuffy relics of Victorian frippery.   In such a setting the play would have been entirely convincing.   We should have found that stockbroker natural who gave ten thousand pounds and the run of his office to his old friend, and secret instructions to his clerk.   Natural, too, would have been the young doctor setting up in practice on the strength of a case of champagne and a stethoscope, of wooden make, productive of dints in the medico's topper.   Entirely natural, finally, would have been that last scene, in which the lovers, unable to find the gas, carry on their tender colloquy by means of matches.   In the day of switches the scene loses all its point.

Left to themselves, the actors played in whatever key took his or her individual fancy.   Mr. Robert Courtneidge, returning to his old love after thirty-five years, was very amusing in the Edward Terry manner. No modernity here, although one suspected the actor of giving a Pirandellish turn to the remark : " Young man, it would have been money in your pocket if you had never been born."   Mr. Holman Clark, to whose whiskers I always look forward as a lover to his mistress, appeared shorn of those adjuncts to natural and legitimate joy. His part in this play is a character part if ever there was one, but Mr. Clark chose, I venture to think wrongly, to play it in the straight, modern, inappropriate way. Piccadilly weepers, Lord Dundrearies, mutton-chops—this delightful artist could have committed no anachronism at which we should have boggled. An august colleague has suggested that Mr. Peter Haddon served his apprenticeship in musical comedy. *De mimimis non curat* Mr. Walkley. I am inclined to think that it is to revue that credit should be given, musical comedy and acting being a contradiction in terms. Mr. Haddon made great play with the Oxford fashion in trousers, though there was little in the text to support a modern skit upon the bagginess of mind which they symbolise so admirably. Mr. Richard Bird, whom I am glad to welcome back from America, has not been spoiled by that continent. He remains likeable. But I suggest that one who is at the end of his financial resources pawns his ring first and his jacket and waistcoat afterwards. Mr. Henry Kendall, as the young doctor, fooled it to the top of his bent in the best Bob Sawyer manner. This was good farce acting of a kind, though the kind was nearer sixty than forty years out of date. Miss Rosaline Courtneidge could not have done any better with her material, and I am content to say that Miss Lottie Venne was, is, and always will be, a dear.

*July* 28.

# " Cæsar and Cleopatra "

## A Play by BERNARD SHAW

### Kingsway Theatre

PANTING Time may not toil after Mr. Shaw in vain, but it is hard for his commentators to do anything else. I suppose the normal conception of virtue is two-fold : doing what we don't like, and not doing what we do like. Or so we might epitomise what the General Confession invites us to say about the devices and desires of our own hearts and our offences against holy law. But Mr. Shaw would compel us to a different conception altogether ; that the virtue of a good man consists not in trying to be good, but in being good from the start. In other words, a leopard is a good leopard according to the number of spots with which he is born, and not according to the efforts he may make to increase spottiness.

Mr. Chesterton has declared his solemn conviction that in taking away moral credit from Jack the Giant Killer " Bernard Shaw in the course of his whole simple and strenuous life was never quite so near to hell." I want to declare my solemn conviction that never in the course of his complicated and strenuous essays in spirituality has Mr. Shaw been nearer Heaven than in a passage in this play. The Queen of Egypt, having hired assassins to kill Pothinus, defends her crime on the grounds of lawful vengeance.

> CLEO : Listen to me, Cæsar. If one man in all Alexandria can be found to say that I did wrong, I swear to have myself crucified on the door of the palace by my own slaves.
>
> CÆSAR : If one man in all the world can be found, now or forever, to *know* that you did wrong that man will have either to conquer the world as I have or be crucified by it.

I take Cæsar's reply to be the noblest utterance, and also the most pregnant and the most dramatic— because of its sudden appeal to the deepest thing in modern consciousness—not only in Mr. Shaw's works, but in the whole range of English literature since Shakespeare. The appeal, of course, is Cæsar's to his modern hearers, not to his interlocutors in the play. Cleopatra probably thought her friend was just blethering.

Mr. Shaw's hero is very perfectly abreast of Mommsen's ; but then so, by the way, was Shakespeare's. Mommsen says that the historian, on those rare occasions when he encounters perfection, can only be silent regarding it. Shakespeare, struck all of a heap by his " noblest man," gives him words which would not be too good for Cæsar's valet. But it takes more than perfection to silence Mr. Shaw—in fact, it eggs him on to go one better, and suggest super-perfection. Cæsar is Mr. Shaw's hero because he is Shavian.    His ideas are unclouded by idealism or any kind of romantic nonsense.    He is, as the German historian points out, a realist and a man of sense.    I sometimes wonder what Mr. Shaw would have made of Brutus and Cassius. The latter, I think, would have won his respect.    But he would have delighted, surely, to pin-prick and deflate that muddle-headed idealist and man of romantic non-sense, Brutus ; and I can imagine a capital scene in which Cæsar's assassin, who could spend the night before the battle of Pharsalia making an abridgement of Pausanias, would have been shown exercising his by-profession as a moneylender, and telling Cicero, who is known to have been his client, that the Roman rate of 10 per cent. was strictly reasonable in view of the risks of the business in general and the uncertainty of the writing profession in particular.

But this is by the way.    It is Cæsar and nobody else who fascinates Mr. Shaw, and one repeats that he has made him too perfect.    He walks the earth, according to one critic, " with a kind of stern levity, like a winged man who has chosen to fold his wings, making the men in front of him feel as if they were made of glass."    This is finely put, but isn't it less a picture of perfect humanity than of perfect inhumanity ?    " I am he," says Cæsar to the Sphinx, " of whose genius you are the symbol : part brute, part woman, and part god—nothing of man in me at all."    And later, on being asked whether Cæsar despairs : " He who has never hoped can never despair."    I take this to be not perfect man, but perfect fish. Cæsar is first cousin to the He-Ancient in *Back to Methuselah* and not even the people who murdered him could have wished him anything worse.

Too much nobility, however, is better than too little, and the play ranks among its author's definitely great achievements. There is not nearly enough of Britannus, that patient, static, and almost ecstatic butt. If Mr. Shaw had been a mediæval stone-mason one feels that every day in the week he would have put in his ten or twelve hours of cheerful grind at the main body of his cathedral, but also that he would have given up his Sundays to working for nix on the gargoyles. Britannus is the unconquerable schoolboy in Shaw making a long nose at everything the British race stands for. Cleopatra in this play does nothing but put out her tongue, and she does it adorably. But the play is not really about her at all. " Cæsar and Mr. Shaw " is its real title, and you could even put *that* the other way round. For, though the play tells us little about Cæsar that we did not know, it tells us a great deal about Mr. Shaw that we might not have guessed.

For once in a way the " expressionist " scenery seemed to me to break down, perhaps because it wasn't expressionist enough. Cleopatra's Palace looked to me to be merely cock-eyed. The second scene had no suggestion of illimitable sky and desert, moonlight, empty space, and emptier melancholy ; and the Sphinx was too patently cut out in white card-board. The sea was as obviously artificial as a modish head of hair, and its waves were pure Marcelle. And if the water was to be formally suggested, why bother about those very realistic grains of rice, or whatever it is that is used to imitate a splash ?   But this play really calls for spectacle and a big stage.   Without these the eye goes hungry, and in the way of mere sound the ear is something starved ; in the matter of words Mr. Shaw is a poet to whom poetry has been denied.   But Mr. Shelving's costumes were entirely lovely.

How about Cæsar ?   I have no desire to belittle Mr. Cedric Hardwicke's earnest and conscientious performance by saying that it was earnest and conscientious, but I do not see that I can go any further in the way of praise.   Mr. Shaw takes his hero for superhuman, and I take him for sub-human ; but super or sub, the quality can only be rendered by an actor possessing that blaze of romantic egotism which is the stock-in-trade of your " great " actor.   There was, however, a good deal of dignity about this Cæsar, and many of his poses were admirable.   Miss Gwen Ffrançon-Davies found in Cleopatra the part for which she was born. Mr. Stanley Lathbury's Pothinus was good, and Mr. Scott Sunderland, made up to look like Taffy in *Trilby*, gave Britannus his maximum phlegm.   Only the Nubians did not quite convince me.   They looked too much like gentlemanly income-tax collectors attending a fancy-dress ball disguised as Gollywogs.   Either a Nubian is naked or he is nothing.

*April* 21.

# "Mrs. Warren's Profession"

## A Play by BERNARD SHAW

### Regent Theatre

Hood's poems are no clamorous expressions of anger at the discrepancies and contrasts of humanity, but plain, solemn pictures of conditions of life, which neither the politician nor the moralist can deny to exist, and which they are imperatively called upon to remedy.—Lord Houghton.

WHEN Margaret Knox attributed her assault upon the policeman to the prayer meeting she put the whole Shavian doctrine in a nutshell. Margaret, you see, knocked out the policeman's teeth in a fit of exactly the same kind of religious exaltation which made Mr. Shaw want to knock the bottom out of slum-landlordism, wage-sweating, and the like. *Mrs. Warren's Profession*, far from being as the censorious of years ago would have had us believe a prose version of Swinburnian roses and raptures, a kind of unmetrical Ode to Déshabille, was a recapitulation in deadly earnest of Thomas Hood's *Song of the Shirt*. It was another plain, solemn picture of conditions calling for amelioration and even the clean sweep. Here, in

1893, was the new broom.    A broom of vision it was, too, prepared to see an Augean mess where a comfortable society beheld only a condition consequent upon sacred economic law.    Not an ideal state of things, perhaps, of the sort desired by Utopians, romantics, and other idealistic wild fowl, but what would you ?    Well, not *that*, at any rate, declared the new broom, preparing to whisk its way into the most horrid corners.

Hercules did not, to our knowledge, make the mistake of being a wit, and therefore had no trouble about getting people to take him and his stables seriously. But there has never been any subject in the heaven above, or on the earth beneath—and even under the earth to the inclusion of tube railways and systems of drainage—upon which Mr. Shaw could refrain from being witty, which is the reason why he has had to wait half a lifetime for recognition as perhaps the greatest moral force of our age.    Again, Shavian morality has always taken some understanding.    It begins with a repudiation of Duty as an obligation inspired by fear, and goes on to the ideal of doing something you desperately want to do instead of something your conscience pushes you into without joy.    Thus Vivie says explicitly that she rather admires Crofts for being strong-minded enough to enjoy himself in his own way and make plenty of money out of his life because he wanted to, instead of loafing around in listless imitation of his class.    Shavian morality is not one of the creeds that refuse and restrain ; it is a call to action and a challenge to all humbugs and hypocrisies.    The

## "Mrs. Warren's Profession"

Shavian religion, as was the later Ibsen's, is based largely upon acceptance of this axiom : actions are to be judged by their effect on happiness, and not by their conformity to any ideal.

Now, it is possible that in 1893 the honest girl of the working class without any special ability had small choice of vocation. Vivie says, with all the intolerance of youth and inexperience, that the poorest girl can choose between rag-picking and flower-selling, and her mother does not even brush away this flimsy argument by asking whether there are enough buyers of flowers to occupy all the nice girls. Mrs. Warren sits down and tells her daughter exactly what happened to two nice girls and two not nice girls. One of the honest creatures worked in a white-lead factory, twelve hours a day, for nine shillings a week, until she died of lead poisoning ; the other married a Deptford labourer, and kept his room and three children neat and tidy on eighteen shillings a week until he took to drink. Whereas Vivie's unrespectable Aunt Lizzie stepped into her carriage at once, and she herself, Vivie's mother, took up the profession we know of as an effective protest against washing glasses behind a bar for fourteen hours a day in return for four shillings a week and board. If actions are to be judged by resulting happiness or misery, which of these women shall we blame ?

The argument went on : It is no use telling poor girls that they ought to prefer dying of lead poisoning to rolling around Hyde Park in a barouche. Make the conditions of wage-earning such that a girl can maintain

231

herself in reasonable comfort by her own industry without selling her affections in the way of marriage or otherwise. Then tell her, if you like, that if she is a good girl she will be happy. But make the social conditions such that she cannot round upon you and point out that all the good girls she knows are hopelessly miserable. And at this point, I think, the validity of the play's argument came to an end even in its own time. Consent to its last ramifications will not be general even to-day.

Now that the improvement in material things has been effected, the centre of the play's interest has shifted from the material condition of the wage-slave to the spiritual state of the slave-driver. Mrs. Warren's second act speech is an economic diatribe ; that in the fourth act is not a philippic, but a justification. What Mrs. Warren says essentially here is that she is more fit for her profession than for any other : " Imagine me in a cathedral town ! Why, the very rooks in the trees would find me out, even if I could stand the dullness of it." This raises the question—whether it is better for a woman who has a genius for brothel-keeping to succeed as a brothel-keeper or fail as a police-woman. Better for the woman is meant, of course, a good Shavian maxim being that if the individual will look after himself we need not bother about the community. Is it better for Mrs. Warren to make use of her evil talents, or to bury them ? But you must add the rider that everybody else is to abandon humbug and use his talent according to his own judgment. Leave out this rider, and the justification of Mrs. Warren makes the play's presentation to-day infinitely less moral than it could have been thirty years ago. There is one great flaw in the piece, which time has not altered, and that is the nature of Mrs. Warren's crime. To sin in one's own person is one thing, to traffic in sin is another. The woman's case is too thin here, and the statement that her creatures were happier than the average bar-maid or the average wife of a Deptford labourer is simply not true.

Mrs. Warren herself is drawn in the round, the rest of the characters are mere intellectual abstractions. Vivie, in so far as she is alive at all, is a prig, Crofts is a sawdust monster, Frank is very little removed from a scatter-brain, and the clergyman and the artist are just not anything at all. But Mrs. Warren, that genial old blackguard, is as much alive as Falstaff. You know where you are with her ; the rest are but phantoms. It would be pleasant to be able to say that the Macdona Players performed the piece adequately. But they did not. The play should really have been presented in the costumes of the early 'nineties, when women who were " loud " dressed loudly. Miss Florence Jackson, condemned to resemble too closely a figment of Miss Connie Ediss's imagination, played her part with understanding, and touched acceptance at the end. Sincerity will out, even in the business of acting. As Vivie Miss Valerie Richards made one wonder whether Meggie Albanesi might not have made some-thing human of this animated brain, while Mr. Charles

Sewell's Crofts behaved like the natural father of one of Mr. G. P. Huntley's comic dudes. Mr. Johnston's Praed attained possibility, but Mr. George Bancroft, after three acts of hopeless struggle against the archness of Frank, accepted defeat in a suiting which called down fire from Heaven. But one felt that the actors knew what they were about. If they did not illuminate the play, at least they did not stand in its light. Stevenson has something about the unconquerable spirit of the man who means execution, and perhaps one could say of these actors that a spirit went out of them which defied indifferent execution.

*September* 28.

NOTE.—I have put this piece into the catalogue of revivals, to which, but for the imbecility of the censorship, it would actually belong.

# "The Madras House"

## A Comedy by HARLEY GRANVILLE-BARKER

### Ambassadors Theatre

HAS anybody noticed, I wonder, that each of
the four married women in this play is an
Awful Warning against marriage ?  First there is
Katherine Huxtable, a British matron bound in triple
hide of ignorance, prejudice and convention.  Second
is Amelia Madras, whose placid obstinacy of self-
martyrdom would drive any man into sin.  More
awful still is Mrs. Brigstock, that embittered, jealous,
charmless spouse with one eye fixed on the main chance
and the other on her husband's discomfort.  Last there is
Jessica Madras, who must come down to the office
instead of telephoning and cannot see why she should
not be taken out to lunch, who feels herself neglected
and chooses her husband's best friend as the repairer of
that neglect.  Jessica has become a familiar figure since
this play was first produced, for in the meantime the
cinema has sprung up, which industry exists, as we all
know, for the explaining of the Jessicas and nobody else.

Yet one would suppose that Mr. Granville-Barker did

not write this play to warn the world against marriage, for in it he says quite a lot of things in favour of that institution, not omitting a good word here and there for polygamy and even polyandry. "Here's a church," said Mr. Wemmick, "let's get married." Mr. Barker would seem to preach that nobody should pass a church without rushing in to espouse some starved damsel from the neighbouring drapery stores. Of course, it really is very awkward when the number of women in any country greatly exceeds the men, and when that country also holds that the present marriage system belongs to the same order of things as gravity and the composition of the air. One wonders whether, fifty years ago, the Huxtable family were quite such a joyless, broken-spirited, dependent lot. I am afraid the answer is yes. But since the war we have changed all that, and it is not to be imagined that six daughters between the ages of nineteen and thirty-nine in a middle-class family would spend all the days of their life in Denmark Hill moping after the men they have failed to attract. To-day, one thinks, each girl would do something either for her living or her self-respect. But nothing of the sort is indicated in Mr. Barker's play. One of these wretched Huxtable girls cherishes a frog, another a geranium, while a third weeps in secret over the collar of a fashionable actor sent home with the laundry by mistake. What a seraglio! And the awful thing is that one feels that these people really did exist. The war has done something if it has done nothing more than liberate them.

Then comes the second act. Was the living-in system in large drapery stores ever quite so bad as it is represented in this play and in some of the novels of Mr. H. G. Wells ? Yes, we are forced to think that it must have been. Has it been altered ? Can it be altered ? Or is Mr. Barker merely rebelling against one of the laws of this world which philosophers have long ago accepted—that life is very pleasant for people who have money, and very unpleasant for those who haven't ? A German philosopher once said to me *à propos* of the Armenian massacres : " If a man will be an Armenian he must know what to expect ! " In the same way if a young woman will be an assistant in a drapery store she, too, must know what to expect. If there is a hell upon earth I imagine that it is surely peopled by the young women who stand for nine mortal hours with swollen ankles behind a counter failing to sell ribbon to other women who think that it does not match, and looking forward to an evening of cocoa and a duenna-ship like that of Miss Chancellor and an old age equally spectral. If living-in in drapery stores is not like that to-day, I shall be glad to hear it.

The first two acts, then, are capital play-writing. They are enthrallingly interesting, and are put to-gether with a sympathy in which there is nothing maudlin. But after them the deluge ! For the action now stops, and Mr. Barker begins to talk through the mouths of half a dozen people sitting round a table. It is always a dangerous sign whenever an author of the Shavian school gets his knees under the mahogany, and Mr. Barker is no exception. Has there ever in the whole of dramatic literature been a greater bore than the American storekeeper in this play ? Mr. Claude Rains did his best to minimise the tedium of that personage, whose original conception is first-class. His mind is as low as a storekeeper can get, yet so smeared over with pretentious moral uplift that he cannot see what complexion the horrid mess really is. But then Mr. Barker couldn't let the idea alone, and began to worry it, saying everything twice over that he might be sure about it himself, and then twice over again so that the audience should make no mistake, and once more for luck. The whole of this act is weariness itself. The fourth act straggles to some sort of an end in the sandy deltas of discussion. But the first and second acts remain fine, and nothing will ever prevent me from going to see half this play whenever and wherever it is produced.

The acting was exceedingly brilliant throughout. Indeed, I do not suppose that a better example of team work has ever been seen upon any stage. Take Miss Frances Ivor, who plays Katherine Huxtable as God made her and not otherwise. You don't argue about a character or a piece of acting like this. There they are like Beachy Head or the Needles. Just as perfect is the Amelia Madras of Miss Irene Rooke. How could any man live for any length of time with a woman for whom no sermon can be too long ? Admiration could be equally divided between the venom of Miss Mary

Barton's Mrs. Brigstock and the vinegar of Miss Agnes Thomas's Miss Chancellor. The bevy of Huxtables was so good that I feel that I must give the names in detail. They are as follows : Christine Jensen, Winifred Oughton, Susan Claughton, Ann Codrington, Marie Ney, and Lois Heatherley. Miss Cathleen Nesbitt and Mr. Allan Jeayes did all that was expected of them according to plan. To conclude, there were three performances of quite remarkable perfection. First, there was that pale Mr. Brigstock of Mr. Stafford Hilliard, so wholly shop-assistant and so little man. Then there was Miss Doris Lytton's bright and cheerful Marion Yates, who had saved three hundred pounds against the time when she was going to have her baby, and did not really see that the affair could be anybody else's business. Last there was Mr. Nicholas Hannen's Philip Madras. I believe it is largely the fault of actors like Mr. Hannen that the stage is so overcrowded. They give one the idea, do such actors, that the business is an easy one in which the greatest duffer cannot fail. The truth, of course, is exactly the contrary, the whole of Mr. Hannen's performance in this piece being a network of precise and careful art.

*December* 1.

# " Iris "

## A Play by A. W. PINERO

### Adelphi Theatre

THAT Sir Arthur Pinero's characters speak with
the tongues of angels, but never, oh never,
with those of men, must be patent, as their author might
put it, to cerebellums of meanest capacity.   When the
embezzling solicitor decamps  Iris Bellamy turns to
Croker Harrington and says, " Do you imagine a
woman can be as self-centred as I have been, pamper
herself as I have done, without meriting chastise-
ment ? "   And the play is hung up for just that second
which it takes us to make the mental correction—
" without deserving punishment."

But if the women are ponderous the men are arch !
Oh, the archness of these elderly, world-wearied inno-
cents !   And their old-fashioned gallantry !   Croker,
discovering his hostess, must say, " Ah, those alabaster
shoulders can belong but to one person."   Then note
the insistence of these parasites upon their social
" rightness."   They exhale Mayfair, and you are to
hear them do it.   How they fawn upon money, and
how much of it they need !   Several hundreds a year ?

Enough to provide a man with gloves and cab fares. The whole conveyed on Mrs. Markham's system of Question and Answer. "What, mamma, is a Club Secretary?" Harry will ask; and later Lucy will desire to know what needy gentlefolk mean by "looking round."

A more grievous charge is that the truth is not told about Iris. Here, I think, we must make the time-allowance. Could, in 1901, the truth have been told in the English theatre about such a character? Fashionable playwriting was then at least fifty years behind fashionable thinking. And if Sir Arthur was always twenty-five years behind current thought, he was at least twenty-five years ahead of his stage. The trumpets of Mr. Shaw's veracity, though blowing vigorously, were as yet but faintly heard; and Sir Arthur may very well have deemed half the truth to be better than no truth at all.

Or we may say that not more than half of what we are told about Iris is falsehood. We are allowed to realise at the end, but not earlier, that morally she does not possess and never has possessed vestige or semblance of backbone. She will not marry a poor man because thereby she must lose the fortune left her by her first husband. When her fortune is gone she will not go with Laurence to his cattle-ranch, because she does not like cattle-ranches. But she will accept Maldonado as a protector, though willing to leave him as soon as the cattle-rancher has prospered. At the end she falls between two stools, going out into the night riding a

241

repentant one of her own. But we realise that the mood will not last, and that May will see her queening it at the opera.

The falsification of *Iris* consists in this, that her degradation is presumed to be the punishment of misdoing, whereas properly, it is nothing of the sort. There is nothing in Iris to degrade ; she is essentially and from the beginning toy and plaything. But Sir Arthur has always set his face against any such assumption. We remember what view Aubrey Tanqueray holds of Paula at Ellean's age. Fanny Sylvain says the same things about Iris. " Even at school there wasn't a girl who wouldn't have sold her little white soul for a caress from Iris." Think now of the enormous pains taken to prop up this falsification. Whereas all the other defalcating solicitor's victims lose the whole of their fortunes Iris is allowed to retain £150 a year. Why ? Because her creator did not want us to read " function " for " punishment," and to realise what she must have done without that pittance. Because we are to weep over the " nobility " of Iris on her knees among her trunks, deciding, " with such a sweet, earnest, helpless, confident look " that for the third-rate boarding-houses of the future her third-best frocks will do. Because she is to draw the first cheque in Maldonado's book for some preposterous act of Quixotism rather than to settle an hotel bill bigger than she reckoned for. Only so could sentimentality's core have been preserved.

And yet *Iris* remains a capital play. You do quite

desperately want to know what A will say next—though it is bound to be couched in terms unknown to the human tongue. And you do very urgently want to know what B is going to do next—though you are aware that it will not be what he would do in real life. In other words, Sir Arthur Pinero in this piece, as in all others, is a master of " situation." Judge *Iris* by what its author set out to do, and it is almost impossible to say that he has not perfectly succeeded. Is there, perhaps, a flaw in the leave-taking scene ? Laurence asks Iris, now poor, to go away with him. Her real reason for refusal is that life even in a filthy *pension* is better than life on a beastly cattle-ranch, and if Sir Arthur were re-writing the piece to-day he might perhaps hint that at the back of her mind is Maldonado. But the reason she gives is that she cannot join the young man until she has proved to herself and him that she can stand poverty. Now I, for one, don't believe that tale, any more than I believe her further story of penurious sojourn in sea-side resorts out of season and Wolverhampton in August. Neither is true even to the fictitious Iris of the play ; both are necessitated by the plot. But once Maldonado has put Iris *dans ses meubles* the play is faultless. Prior to 1900 Sir Arthur would not have allowed even half the truth to escape him. The century turned, he lets Truth in half way through the evening.

Miss Gladys Cooper, moving from strength to strength, plays Iris with extraordinary naturalness and a great deal of power. You feel that she could rise to the real Iris, and that only the play keeps her down. The essence of Maldonado is repellence, of Mr. Ainley, attraction. This allowance made, the part is rendered with an intelligence approaching virtuosity. The rest of the cast is good, but not unbearably so.

*March* 21.

# "Old Heidelberg"

## From the German of W. MEYER-FORSTER

### Garrick Theatre

I KNOW quite well what I am expected to say about this piece, and I have not the least intention of saying it. Let austerer critics fulminate against *Old Heidelberg's* tedium, its unheavenly length and treacly sentiment—these faults are admitted. The short-winded German is yet to be born ; and to endure three hours and a half of Herr Meyer-Forster is to be held too long in bondage to a fifth-rate mind. But your fifth-rater may have some inkling of a first-rate idea, and among melancholies nostalgia holds high place. The reader who should deny this has forgotten his Loti.

We are always being told that criticism is largely a personal matter, and this must be my excuse here. I liked *Old Heidelberg* on Thursday evening last because I liked it on a Thursday afternoon a quarter of a century ago. The company performing the piece there was a German one, and contained at least two very fine actors. The theatre was small and intimate, and the play was taken at a tremendous rate. I had not long

245

left school, had paid my first visit as an old boy, and
tasted some—though in the absence of a Kathie not all
—of the bitterness of the German princeling. I had
successfully worried through *Werther*, and wallowed
in Massenet's setting of that sentimental masterpiece.
I had actually spent a month in Heidelberg, and was
altogether as good a little German as a certain school of
political thought, popular in those pre-war days, could
have desired. In addition, the afternoon was hot, the
pit of the theatre sweltering, and I had played truant
from a disgusting apprenticeship to the business of
selling calico. How, then, not to like the piece? The
Kail-yard school of fiction was very much in vogue,
and this excellent example of Sauerkraut was admirably
timed. In short, I relished it all immensely. And I
am sentimentalist enough to insist upon relishing it
to-day.

Perhaps one need not have gone so far afield as
Pierre Loti to find a champion for the nostalgia *motif*.
The author of *Tom Brown's School Days* would have
done just as well, and probably better. The one really
first-class scene in this play is the opening of the
epilogue, rather pretentiously called a fifth act. Karl
Heinrich revisits Heidelberg after two years, and
receives the chilly welcome accorded to a potentate.
The students form up in line, salute him, and sing
dirges over his living body. Even his beer-mug must
be of another shape and material. One thinks the
prince himself is something to blame. He makes no
protest, has no " Hang it all, you fellows . . . ! " A

far finer effect could have been got out of the failure of German good-fellowship to defeat nervousness in the matter of *lèse-majesté*. But the root-idea of the prince's melancholy is good enough, as those will know who remember Tom's feelings upon revisiting Rugby.

In the matter of Kathie, it is a little difficult to believe that the hearts of princes are allowed to break as easily as commoner ware. It is true that Karl Heinrich had to contract a diplomatic alliance. Still, one thinks that seccotine in the way of morganatic marriage might have been applied. And if Kathie could not get out of that entanglement with the Viennese pastrycook, was there no need of Lebkuchen at the palace ? But Karlsburg's morality was doubtless as strict as Ruritania's, and so the play must end with Rassendyl eating out his heart and Flavia secretly determining to send her Royal lover a pound of marzipan every Christmas Day. But poor Kathie is altogether a bit of a stumbling-block to English minds. A trip to Paris with your Oxford landlady's daughter is simply " not done " ; in Germany we may believe that another code prevails. The whole idea of the Gretchens and the Kathies, their very reason for existence, is to provide sluicings of sentiment and romantic passion, followed by Niagaras of remorse. Love is no part of your Oxford undergraduate's life, or should not be ; 'tis, conjoined with poetry and beer, your Heidelberg student's whole existence. Therefore let the story pass. It is human, which is more than can be said for the fashionable American comedy of sentiment.

The play was moderately well done at the Garrick. It was much too long, and should have been cut by a full hour. As it was, the evening was half spent before Mr. Novello was called upon to begin acting, which in the end he did gracefully and at times movingly, even to the point of surviving a uniform reminiscent of a municipal bandsman from Southend. Was there perhaps a shade too much Latin sophistication about his pretty wistfulness ? No actor can perpetually endure those " patent double million magnifyin' gas microscopes of hextra power," as Sam Weller might call the cinema's arcs, and preserve Teutonic depths of innocence. But on the emotional side Mr. Novello registered a distinct advance. The Kathie of Miss Dorothy Batley was a clever simulation of the little goose of tradition. Mr. E. W. Thomas hardly got out of the old tutor all that there is in the part, in which both the German actor and the late J. D. Beveridge were magnificent. As the dull and pompous valet Mr. Ernest Benham achieved too great a degree of verisimilitude, thus transgressing the rule that stage bores should not distress the audience. Those who saw Mr. Reginald Dane in *Polly Preferred* will know how amusing this long part might have been made. Mr. Ian O. Will was very amusing as a college " Gyp," but I thought that the best performance was given by Mr. Alexander Onslow, who, of all the cast, alone achieved the guttural both in accent and mood. This despite, or perhaps because of, the fact that he was suffering from a terrible cold.

The audience received the revival with every mark of favour, and I here confess my personal affection for the old piece. But let not the modern kail-yarder who should be contemplating an " Old Aberdeen " look for similar indulgence.

*February* 5.

# " Kismet "

## A Play by EDWARD KNOBLOCK

### New Oxford Theatre

SHALL it be confessed that for the ten days which, to any right-thinking mind, constitute Easter my heart was not in Shaftesbury Avenue ? Yes ; for not only is open confession good for the soul, but it is also prevents the ignominy of discovery. Nor yet was that heart in the Highlands ; but half way, and divided between Windermere and Doncaster. The latter principally, for it is in that town and at Easter that the harness horses and harness ponies, which later are to delight us at Richmond and Olympia, make their first bow of the season. Just as a new play may be " tried out " at Brighton, Glasgow, or Liverpool, so the Olympia champion gives a foretaste of his quality in those bleak Glasgow paddocks. But I must draw rein here—this article must, shall, and will deal with the theatre.

Now I am conscientiousness itself. And therefore were a number of new plays, a volume of Lessing's dramatic criticism, and a thoroughly German study of the divergence between Brunetière's *View of Rosen-*

*crantz* and Croce's *Aspects of Guildenstern* packed into
a certain despatch case which, it was intended, should
accompany the heavier luggage.   But at Euston the
awful discovery was made that the whole caboodle had
been left behind.   No papers were published on the day
of my journey and the bookstalls were closed.   Till
Rugby I must meditate on the state of the English
theatre, and wonder why it is that in London good plays
do so much less well than middling ones ; while, if a
play be only bad enough, there is as like as not " a
fortune in it."   I was to be a little enlightened in this
most sad matter before we got to Crewe.   For a
fellow-pasenger, seeing my plight, proposed to lend me
a novel.   The offer was gladly accepted.

Wild horses will not drag from me the real name of
the book or its author.   Sufficient that it was published
early in 1914, and in eleven years has gone through
nine editions.   *That's for Remembrance* seemed to me
to be utter " tripe "—if the vulgarism be permitted—
not to be ironed out into any semblance of good writing.
The first page alone cried aloud for seventeen correc-
tions !   And then there was the plot !   Only Boshington could have invented that working engineer
with the hands of a navvy, the body of Apollo and face
of Narcissus, the mind of a Huxley, the religious con-
victions, or their opposite, of a Bradlaugh, the stainless
soul of a Galahad, and the moody, yet eloquent,
silences of Godfrey Tearle.   Only Boshington could
have composed that widow emerging from unhappy
wifehood more virginal than Perdita and more provoca-

tive than Beatrice. And when, on the top of a heavy dinner, Lady Thingumbob sang one of those songs of which the secret, though lost to Schubert, Brahms, and Wolf, has always lain open to your novelist—" an air at once languorous yet throbbing with concealed passion, dim with the hush of cloisters, yet gay with mordant mockery "—when our cantatrice, having finished her ditty, unlatched the casement so that the moon fell on her argent breast, diamanté corsage, and gleaming arms, what, I ask, could our poor engineer hiding in the bushes on the other side of the drive do but deliver up his manly soul ? But—alas for the careless fellow !—had he not the previous afternoon given tea and succour to a poor girl of his own class who had fallen off her bicycle and sprained her ankle ? And had not Lady Thingumbob surprised the innocent pair and, after the manner of the " right " people, drawn the wrong conclusion ? What, therefore, could her ladyship do but repulse the engineer when his miraculously successful invention enabled him to lay not only his heart but a million pounds at her noble feet ? So the poor fellow, out of spite and chivalry mixed, must go back to his inexpert bicyclist with the cheap hat and shoddy manners, and marry her out of hand. There was a lot more story to follow with which I will not weary the reader.

My whole point is that though I could not defend a single chapter, paragraph, or even sentence of this monstrous piffle, I found it entirely engrossing. The book was beneath any kind of critical consideration, yet

I could not, as they say, put it down. Nor yet could I attribute my fascination to the absence of any other literature. For since at Carnforth I must yield the masterpiece up to its owner, and though my host's library at Windermere possesses all the treasures of the language from Pope to Bradley, yet must I instruct the local bookseller to procure me *That's for Remembrance* without an unnecessary second's delay. I felt I could not endure until I knew "how it ended." The moral? Well, this I take to be it, if any there be. The moral is that in the theatre many plays please which are to be defended upon no ground other than the simple one that it is pleasure which they give. If you cannot leave the playhouse until you have heard what retort A. has to make to that nasty remark of B.'s, and if you feel that, for the moment, the most important thing in the world is to know whether C. will fall into the pit digged for him by D., and once in how he will clamber out—if a play excites in you those two emotions, then it is a good play, whatever anybody may say to the contrary. It doesn't matter if A., who is supposed to be a duke, talks like a hairdresser. It doesn't matter if D. in actual life would never have dug the pit, or if C., by using ordinary common sense, would have run no danger of falling into it. Half the art of drama is the art of arousing curiosity—though finer names are given to it by the high-brows—and the other half is satisfying it. A play is a bad play if you do not care whether you stay to the end of it or not. I like that story of the playgoer in Madrid who, when the drama was at the height of its supposed tension, groped for his hat, rose in his stall, and, stifling a yawn, said casually to his neighbours, " Well, shall we be going ? " One of the dangers of criticism is that the critics are too prone to leave what I call the " curiosity-factor " out of consideration. That is why so many simple people look upon critics as offensive meddlers. They, not being forced by too much playgoing into the hypercritical attitude, want to see the end of almost any play. Therefore, almost any play is a good play. There is a good deal to be said for this point of view, and if this critic seem occasionally to err on the side of leniency, will readers note, please, that this is a point of view which he declines to lose sight of ?

*Kismet*, very happily and successfullly revived at the New Oxford, is a good play in the sense that the stories in the *Arabian Nights* are good stories. There is, perhaps, only one moment of drama, which occurs when the Beggar lifts up the hand and arm of the drowning Wazir, and tells that scoundrel all that every child has longed to tell him since the beginning of the tale. It has been well said that all stories of hidden treasure must end with the discovery of the *cache*. In the same way it is essential that the Beggar shall return to begging at the end, and his daughter espouse the Caliph, whom she took to be little better than a donkey-boy. Poetic justice is not necessarily a morbid, catastrophic affair, and if sophisticated hearts do not beat as fast at the *dénouement* as some others, it is, after all, their loss. The scenery and dresses throughout the production are of unending delight, and the music shows Mr. Norman O'Neill at his most Baghdacious. The best performances are those of Miss Mary Clare and Mr. Robert Harris. As the man fra' Persia Mr. Livesey is good, though he does not drown recollection of Mr. Asche. Miss Elissa Landi is so pretty and so artless that her friends are perhaps justified in deeming criticism of her art to be irrelevant. *Kismet* is a play for lovers of beauty half naked and quite unashamed.

*April* 22.

# Melodrama

# "The Show"

## A Melodrama by JOHN GALSWORTHY

### St. Martin's Theatre

MR. GALSWORTHY bears a certain re-
semblance to the heroines of Miss Dell.
He likes having his feelings lacerated as they their
bodies. He has a passion for the ill-used. His is the
head upon which all the martyrdoms of the world are
come, and the eyelids are not at all weary.

The heroine of his new play is a young married
woman seeking escape from the consequences of her
husband's suicide and her own antecedent indiscretions,
and accompanied in her flight by those vultures, the
police and the sensational Press. Mr. Galsworthy
tackles both birds manfully, but unfortunately—if a
change of metaphor be permitted—gets the pig by the
wrong ear. He shows his policeman vastly exceeding
the scope of his duties, and the journalist risking the
loss of his job by a wildly improbable exercise of dis-
cretion and taste. One simply doesn't believe that any
detective, having assured himself that Colonel Morecombe's death was suicide, would proceed to an inquisition of Mrs. Morecombe's relations with Geoffrey

Darrel, proved to have been elsewhere at the time of the shooting, or that he would have burgled Darrel's house, or held him up and gone over his pockets in search of incriminating love-letters. The police, as Hedda Gabler might have remarked, don't do such things. And what kind of journalist is he who would not want a photograph of the chair in which the dead man shot himself, and of the Colonel as a little boy in knicker-bockers bowling his first hoop ?

The first act is entirely devoted to this police inquisition. The maidservant admits to having posted a letter written by the Colonel half an hour before he shot himself. This letter is missing, and the detective is of opinion that it must have been addressed to Darrel. We, in the audience, share that opinion, and prepare ourselves for the drama of remorse impinging upon guilty passion. We gather that the coming together of the lovers had been condoned by the explicitly stated fact of the husband's coolness towards his wife and his refusal of children. We are prepared, therefore, to see the remorse *motif* elaborated by a full-dress debate as to the validity of such condonation. But in the second act the journalist starts another hare. He has discovered that the Colonel, on his side, entertained relations with a little waitress. Can it be that the letter was addressed to her ? How far does the exist-ence of this relationship justify that other ? For how much did some sudden realisation of his wife's unfaith-fulness, and the blow struck at conscience by some lightning-flash apprehension of his own, count in the

husband's decision to take his life ?    At the time when
these discords should begin to resolve themselves the
play unaccountably fritters itself away.    A fire-eating
Colonel and an over-bearing old lady, father-in-law and
mother of the dead man, now present themselves.    They
are arrant snobs both, whose minds are solely bent upon
hushing up the affair.    For the agony which must
always precede suicide neither of them, apparently, has a
thought.    The third act is one large red-herring.

It turned out now that the famous letter was
addressed to a naval lieutenant who had been best man
at Colonel Morecombe's wedding.    In it Morecombe
explained that since his marriage he had, unknown to
his wife, twice gone off his head.    (How one keeps a
little thing like that from one's helpmate is a minor
puzzle.)    In view of this disability he had refused
children, while keeping his wife in the dark as to the
reason.    Here Mr. Galsworthy plunged us back into
the Middle Ages, or say, 1860, when a wife was
deemed a chattel devoid of understanding.    Now of
two things one.    If the play was to be the tragedy of a
man whose mind is giving way, then our interest should
have been focussed on the madman and his relation to
the other characters.    If the drama was to be one of
moral action and reaction attending the failure in
responsibility to each other of a group of people, then
we should not have as climax the sudden starting of the
entirely irrelevant madness *motif*.

Probably Mr. Galsworthy had neither theme in
mind.    Probably he set out to depict the exhibition

which people make of themselves when their intrigues become exposed to the light of day. He wanted to show us, I imagine, not so much the dirtiness of the linen as the insistent way in which those who must wash it in public demand to be screened. But did not Mr. Galsworthy see that whilst a more or less perfunctory exposition of some set of scandalous bones would suffice for a moralist chiefly interested in the decencies or indecencies with which those bones are coffined and interred, the public, on the other hand, would want to know all about the skeleton, and how it came to be a skeleton, and have no other care at all ? The dramatist was interested in his moral, the audience in as much of the story as it was allowed to get hold of. The play failed, then, because the author had not got hold of a good story.

But I am by no means sure that Mr. Galsworthy had got hold of a particularly good moral. There is a case for the presentation with reasonable limits of all the facts connected with sudden death. Reasonable publicity is a safeguard against crime, and the conduct of the journalist in this play was unexceptionable. Mr. Galsworthy made a mistake in attacking reasonable publicity. What he should have attacked was that unreasonable sensation-mongering which seeks to present degenerate and criminal lunacy as romance. For that lowest kind of journalism, which is not bounded by the necessity for safeguards but goes on to pander to perverted curiosity, Mr. Galsworthy has in this piece no lash. And the playwright, in my humble opinion, lets off the newspaper proprietor a great deal too easily. Of course, the newspapers which live by filth revel in filth. It would be unreasonable to expect them to do anything else, since it leads to dividends in the present and a peerage in the future. Mr. Galsworthy lays the blame for liking filth on human nature, and again he is wrong. Human nature, in these matters, is exactly as low as the newspaper proprietor would have it. Yet to have made the moral better would not have made the play good. The old star was there, the old hitch was there, but alas, the wagon was to seek.

How is it, by the way, that Mr. Galsworthy can never draw anybody possessing an income of more than three pounds a week without making him, or her, entirely objectionable from every point of view ? The soldier's mother and father-in-law are two arrant snobs caring nothing whatever for what their son and son-in-law may have suffered, but everything for what their neighbours are going to think about it all. But then most of the humanity in this piece seems to me to have gone astray. Take the Colonel's wife. She and her husband had long ceased to live together, and she was passionately in love with the young gentleman in the nicely cut brown suit. What on earth was there for her to become so tragically grieved about when her husband, too stupid to allow her to divorce him, did the one thing which was going to make her life happy ever after ? There is no suggestion in the play that she suffered any sudden revulsion of feeling. Then take the little waitress, the Colonel's friend, who dropped her aitches but scorned to pick up an allowance. Happy Mr. Galsworthy to see the world through such rose-tinted spectacles !

Everything possible was done for the ancestors by Miss Haidée Wright and Mr. Felix Aylmer. Mr. Ian Hunter and Miss Mollie Kerr played the lovers as stage tradition ordains that lovers must be played. That is to say, they held colloquy nose to nose, standing so close that they could not possibly look into each other's eyes without squinting. That the wife should have been so tragically miserable when the husband did the one thing which could make her happy is to be accounted among the more esoteric flutterings of your noble goose. Mr. Leslie Banks, as the detective, put up a frightening performance. He reminded me of the man at the dinner party who, entering upon a discussion, propounded some theory. " Sir," said his neighbour, "I apprehend you !" The wretched man fled. I am persuaded that half the audience watched Mr. Banks in terror. What warrant might not the over-bold fellow produce next ? Miss Hermione Baddeley portrayed the little waitress with great effect. Miss Eileen Sharp and Mr. Aubrey Mather contributed between them three excellent little character sketches, and Mr. Ben Field strove hard to make us believe that Mr. Galsworthy's jokes were really funny. But all this brave acting came to little, the one cheerful moment of the evening being when Mr. Ian Hunter bounced into the coroner's court with a pair of brand new yellow gloves.

*July* 1.

# "The Tyrant"

## A Romantic Drama by RAFAEL SABATINI

### New Theatre

MR. LANG has a fondness for novelist-play-wrights. Regrettable lack of familiarity with Mr. Sabatini's stories prevents me from saying with certainty that they include *The Tyrant*. But they ought to. This not very satisfactory play would probably make an excellent historical romance. In that medium there is scope to paint the times ; the writer's page should, indeed, be stiff with antique jewels and brocades. But the dramatist who fills his scenes with minor personages flourishing obsolete weapons and trailing " period " gowns runs a serious risk.

Much art and practice are required to ensure that the background in plays of this sort shall remain background, and not become the piece itself. A good way is to take some significant figure, not necessarily a known historical personage, but an individual who gives the " note " of the times. When Scribe and Legouvé had finished the first draft of *Adrienne Lecouvreur* they were not perfectly satisfied. Something was wrong, and they could not find that something. They consulted Mahérault, a politician with a passion for the play. " You are a character short," was his dictum. Scribe scratched his head ; already his personages were tumbling over each other. " How and where can I add ? " he asked. " Don't add," was the reply. " Take out half a dozen nobodies and put in an Abbé." It was this Abbé who gave the play its eighteenth century note.

Now Mr. Sabatini had at hand Macchiavelli, in whom might have been visibly symbolised the craft and the power and the intellect of Florence in the late fifteenth and early sixteenth centuries. (Be sure that if ever Mr. Shaw sets out to write a play about the Borgias he will end by writing one about Niccolò Macchiavelli.) What does Mr. Sabatini do with this great figure ? Nothing. He reduces him to lackey's level and fobs him off with a single platitude. And in his place we are to listen at enormous length to the meaningless plottings and counter-plottings of that undistinguished factotum, Prince Ercole Sinibaldi.

I submit that if you could recreate in the flesh Queen Elizabeth and Shakespeare, Henry VIII. and Wolsey, Abraham Lincoln and Seward, and bid them reproduce on the stage conversations which they once actually held, you would not receive the impression that either the personages or the talk were real. You would not get, say from Lincoln, his essential Lincoln-ness to the degree which Mr. Drinkwater contrives. But there is a more important point still, which is this : that each personage being supremely aware of his own times he would not deem it necessary to interpret them to his interlocutor. Now the whole art and contrivance of historical playwriting consists in putting into the mouth of the historical personages dialogue of two kinds —dialogue so distilled that it shall give the impression of real people talking, and dialogue so fulfilled that it shall convey to the spectator the sense of the period which the speaker innocently takes for granted.

Mr. Shaw calls his Warwick and the rest unconscious of the *peculiarities* of the Middle Ages, which is only another way of saying that they were supremely conscious of the normalities of the time. The historical playwright has, then, the choice of two ways. After endowing his characters with a sufficing, articulate consciousness of their own period, he leaves it to them either (1) to explain their attitude to another century, or (2) evince so much awareness of their own that the audience cannot help doing the sum in discrepancy for themselves. But in each case the endowment of consciousness is the all-important matter.

It is clear, then, that the playwright who would create in us the illusion of, say Cesare Borgia or Macchiavelli, must do two things. First, he must ensure that his character shall be flesh and blood and not a mere costumier's block, and of such authenticity that we believe him to be *the* Borgia or *the* Macchiavelli. Next he must show him conscious of Middle Italy round about 1500. What the playwright must *not* do is to make Borgia mumble over the body of some golden-haired ninny that " Love has Conquered."

267

This for two reasons—first, that Borgia would never have said it, and, second, because the consciousness behind such an utterance betrays, not Florence in 1500, but Los Angeles in 1925. I venture to say, with all respect, that the consciousness behind the whole of *The Tyrant* is that of the modern film.

Compare Mr. Sabatini's treatment of Macchiavelli with that of another writer. Mr. Wells describes how, when *The Prince* was being written, Macchiavelli went about his personal affairs, saw homely neighbours, gossiped in the shop of Donato del Corno. In the evening he returned to his study :—

> At the entrance he pulled off his peasant clothes, covered with the dust and dirt of that immediate life, washed himself, put on his " noble court dress," closed the door on the world of toiling and getting, private loving, private hating, and personal regrets, sat down with a sigh of contentment to those wider dreams. I like to think of him so, with brown books before him lit by the light of candles in silver candlesticks, or heading some new chapter of *The Prince*, with a grey quill in his clean, fine hand.

This picture has the stamp of truth upon it, whereas Macchiavelli in the play has the stamp of the contrary quality. That great man was always a great man to himself, and so he must be exhibited to us. To show what he may have been to his times, and to show no more, is to do the greatest possible violence to any truth worth having. Mr. Sabatini's Macchiavelli moves through this play with the queasy air of a waiter at a night club, whose business it is to keep an eye on possible police and whose hand is neither fine nor clean. I agree that the best of Macchiavelli's fame is posthumous. But he was never a nobody, slinking about Borgia's Court like a second murderer who has not washed his face for a week.

But even along his own lines the author has not done too well. Cesare Borgia, proof against frontal attack by virtue of a shirt of mail, is to be overcome by guile. Whose ? Obviously a woman's. What woman ? Obviously the noble daughter of that lord whose town is up in arms against the cut-throat and the poisoner. This story may possibly be junior to the everlasting hills, but that depends upon the age of the hills. Anyhow, the serpent caught in its own toils is always good fun. But why did not Mr. Sabatini set about the tale of Lea's tortured heart with greater vigour, and earlier on in the evening ? The great scene in *Fédora* —the classic play on this theme—occurs when the avenger-temptress is torn between two passions. She has feigned love, only to find that it is become real. Sardou, of course, was your man for squeezing the last drop of subtlety and finesse out of a " situation," and, plentifully aided by Sarah Bernhardt, he made a magnificent thing out of the scene in which Fédora utilised the real love, against which she was still struggling, to make the feigned love convincing.

Mr. Sabatini's Lea neither feels nor feigns. The first act is occupied with her more or less perfunctory offer of self-sacrifice. Cesare does not appear here. In the second act all that happens is that Cesare shows himself to be upon the whole a rather likeable young man, while Lea indicates that in her view he is, as our friends say, " some baby." In the third act Lea surrendered to the Borgia with a minimum of fuss, and, after a pudic lowering and raising of the curtain, mentioned casually that if he went out by the garden he would be murdered according to plan. Whereupon Cesare, who had arranged matters otherwise, made his mistress a low bow, went into the garden, collected his men who had settled with Lea's little lot, formed them into fours, and marched them off to the capture of Lea's home-town. Nothing flatter or tamer than this scene could possibly be imagined. In the end Lea drank the poison intended for Cesare, who promptly dropped to his knees saying that she was a good girl and Love had Conquered.

It is curious how tenderly this family has always fared at the hands of great actors. Bernhardt, when she played Hugo's Lucrèce, made her a figure of piety martyrised by a complex. Cesare, in the present play, is not the Neil Cream of our own times put back into his mediæval splendour, but a drawing-room scoundrel, the villain of schoolgirl romance. Our own Gilderoy, the Scotch outlaw, who when Peg Cunningham surrounded her house with fifty soldiers turned on his betrayer and ripped up her belly with a hanger, was made of more Italian stuff.

Mr. Matheson Lang endowed Cesare with a

princely bearing and a mellifluous voice. There being nothing for him to act he spent most of the time walking about the stage sniffing at a flower. Miss Isobel Elsom had little to do, and did little.

*March* 18.

# "Ordeal"

## A Melodrama by DALE COLLINS

### Strand Theatre

READERS will probably remember the passage
in Rudyard Kipling's story in which McPhee,
or some other Scotsman, defends his integrity as a seaman. " Losh, mon, what's her virgeenity to a lassie ? "
The answer comes pat. " The world and a'. But,
mon, what are we doing at oor time o' life talking aboot
virgeenity ? " The story comes into my mind in
connection with Mr. Dale Collins's *Ordeal*. It may
be that a hard-bitten dramatic critic of the male per-
suasion is not a fitting person to weigh up the more
recondite emotions of the female bosom. Would it
really have been better for Miss Viola Thorpe that she
should fall into the jaws of the waiting shark rather
than into the arms of the ruffianly steward of the very
mediocre sailing yacht *Spray* ?

The present critic, humbly conscious of his grosser
masculinity, ventures to recall some very sensible
observations made by Claudio to the priggish Isabella
upon like occasion. The weariest and most loathed
worldly life, says he, is a paradise to what we fear of

death. Precisely. Claudio would have married all
three witches in *Macbeth*, and Hecate to boot, rather
than have his right hand chopped off, let alone his head
And so would I, or any man who puts a sane value upon
life and refuses to let any single one of the functions of
Nature override all the others. Who knows countess
so comatose, duchess so decayed, or hag so haggard that
he would not prefer her to a waiting shark ? But the
female view in this matter may be one of greater nicety.
There was once a pernickety Picard, or so Montaigne
tells us, " who being upon the scaffold ready to be
throwen downe, there was a wench presented unto him,
with this offer that if hee would marrie her, his life
should be saved, who after he had a while beheld her,
and perceiving that she halted, said hastily : '*Away
away, good hangman, make an end of thy business, she
limps !* ' "

Ted, the steward, was not by any means so repulsive
a fellow as, say Quilp, or Uriah Heep, or Stevenson's
Huish in *The Ebb Tide*. It is true that he had only
one ear, lost probably in the same way in which
Mr. Robey's lady-friend lost hers—pike-fishing. It is
true that if one is to play the Roman daughter the
oppressor may as well have his proper complement of
ears and noses. The matter is of first-class importance,
inasmuch as the fair Viola insists more upon Ted's
shortcomings in natural beauty than upon her own
superfluity in natural piety. Now, shall we clear our
minds of cant for a moment ? Shall we ask ourselves
what would have been Viola's attitude if the sacrificial

273                                                    T

demand had been made by her husband's good-looking
gentleman friend ? Would there then have been
question of sharks ? Would not Viola have donned a
tea-gown of the kind Bernhardt kept for the third act
of *La Tosca*, and, vowing she would ne'er consent,
consented with a remark to the effect that mid-Pacific
is, after all, mid-Pacific ; that the naughty fellow
mustn't expect her to receive him at her husband's
house in Curzon Street ; and that the most he must
expect henceforward will be a frigid bow at the Horse
Show ? My personal and private opinion of Viola is
that she was a complete hypocrite and humbug. Little
Dorothy, the ninny, had all the ninny's sincerity and a
good deal of Isabella's ruthless egotism. Yet when it
came to the point she saw that to send her lover to the
shark was just nonsense, and that to yield to the
ruffian's demand was the plainest of common sense.
And, very much to my surprise, the ninny abandoned
her ninnyishness and said she would do what she
obviously must.

The piece is exciting in ways other than the sentimental, for which I am afraid I am grown a trifle too
old. I should like to believe that this Steward, who
obviously receives good pay and can presumably afford
to cut a dash with expensive ladies during his on-shore
leaves—I should like to believe that Ted is so much
moved by a golden-haired chit that he murders the
yacht's captain and consents to the boat being driven
hundreds of miles out of its course, so that in mid-
ocean he may wreak his wicked will. If I could have

believed this, I should have got the same amount of enjoyment out of the play as your anæmic little nursemaid gets out of her " Lily of the Valley " library of threepenny novelettes. It is not to be denied that the ladies in the audience did get something of this simple satisfaction, one who sat next to me experiencing all the emotions of a jelly in August. She shook and wobbled and sank lower and lower in her seat till I became quite apprehensive, covering her face with her hands as each rapeful moment approached and then asking me, an entire stranger, whether she had missed anything. For myself, I spent most of the time devising plans whereby two unarmed men and three women might have made a better shot at outwitting a madman armed with a couple of revolvers. Even as it was, however, the fighting tactics of the piece were, to my way of thinking, a great deal more exciting than the passionate strategy.

One thought that the characters in *Ordeal* were less well read than their author. If Paul Thorpe, the yacht's owner, had smoked one or two of those excellent cigars over a copy of Mr. Conrad's *Typhoon*, he would have learned that the middle of the Pacific Ocean, entire absence of wind, oppressive heat, and distant thunder make up a concatenation of some foreboding. (Even Vasey Howard, whom one would not have suspected of reading anything, might have heard of the calm before the storm.) If the crew had read their *Treasure Island*—but how should they, seeing that the fastidious owner had chosen to sail with a Dane, a dago, a wholly illiterate Irishman, and a nigger ?—they would have foreseen the necessity of overpowering John Silver before he got too big for his boots. If they had known their Quiller-Couch they would never have allowed the Steward to trick them into making off in the open boat. In a play of this sort it seems to me that the plot should be water-tight.

And now we come to the deaf old lady, that pillar of the *ancien régime*, ready to answer the mob-cry of " To the guillotine ! " with a defiant " On y va, canaille ! " To the old woman the Steward and his kind are *canaille*. In fact, it is her scorn which brings about this villain's overthrow. Ted is drunk with power, and reels off a comminative rhapsody threatening everybody on board. But the old lady suddenly hurling " Steward ! " at him, thus throwing in his face that essential subserviency which cannot stand access of authority, and his back being incautiously set against a gap in the taff-rail, he falls overboard, to the general relief and rejoicing.

On the whole an interesting play, suffering from a superfluity of *motifs* in the musical sense. There is the " better man in an emergency " theme ; there is the mutiny and counter-mutiny theme ; there are the questions of class-conflict and the extent to which those two upright Britons, Thorpe and Howard, would have put forward Claudio's view of the matter. One rather hankered after a tragedy of mass-consciousness after the manner of *The Hairy Ape*, or ironic comedy in the vein of *Boule de Suif*. Mr. Collins may reply that these wildfowl were not his game, and that he aimed at simple melodrama for simple playgoers. In this he has certainly succeeded.

The piece was very well acted. Mr. Lyn Harding, as Ted, was mad, but not more than north-north-west, and he very discreetly tempered the wind of the Steward's brutality to the shingled locks of a delicate audience. But why does this actor allow his name to be printed on the programme in blacker type than those of Mr. Felix Aylmer who was extremely good—when he is otherwise ?—and of a young actor unknown to me, Mr. George Curzon, who did quite remarkably well. Miss Haidée Wright was the deaf old lady who finally overcame the madman out of sheer moral superiority. This actress can get as much emotion out of ten minutes as anybody living, but two hours of the same emotion has not got one much further. I think it is because Miss Wright starts on too high a note, and you get tired even of top Fs if the singer never gives you anything else. Miss Madeleine Seymour was good ; and palely good, too, was Miss Jane Welsh as the ninny. Mr. Donald Walcott, as a nigger deck-hand, was more like a nigger than anybody I have ever seen, and he acted very well, too. But why was not this actor allowed to take his call with all the others ? To invite a coloured gentleman to perform and then exclude him from the applause is an unpleasant snobbism.

*May* 19.

# " The River "

## A Play by PATRICK HASTINGS

### St. James's Theatre

M R. SOMERSET MAUGHAM, asking recently for a definition of the " commercial " theatre, said that he did not see that a play was any the worse because a great many people liked seeing it instead of a few. It isn't. Plays for the precious few are generally no more than precious. When a critic says that a piece belongs to the " commercial " theatre, he means that the playwright has written something which he knows to be untrue because he is afraid the truth will have a thinning effect upon the audience. Let me take an instance from one of Mr. Maugham's own plays. *Our Betters*, like the Battle of Waterloo, was a magnificent success, but it was also, as the Duke observed, " a damn'd near thing." A shade less of wit, a shade less of brilliance in the impudent solution, and the crowd might have been scared away. A playwright of less courage than Mr. Maugham, fearing to snatch at the big prize, would have tacked on a safe " commercial " ending. Lady

George Grayston's husband would have divorced her at the very moment chosen by her American friend for a long-foreseen bankruptcy, and Lady George, exchanging shimmering silver for penitential voile, would have taken the second of two steerage-tickets for Alaska, murmuring that love is dearer than pearls.

Sir Patrick Hastings is too successful a lawyer to despise the successful theatre, and too astute an advocate to believe in the validity of the sentimental side of *The River*. Did, even so long ago as 1915, any young woman, not being an imbecile, allow herself to be tricked into a villain's flat at midnight ? No. Did Lothario, however sombre a fellow, hold so gloomy a view of any soldier-husband's chance of " getting through " that he would risk taunting him in the trenches with a precise and detailed letter ? No. Did any husband return without leave and kill the lover in circumstances of apparent maximum provocation ? It is possible. Did any wife, to save her husband's neck, swear that she had been consistently faithless ? Very likely. But if Mary at the trial really lied like the blackest of the black, would not counsel have explained to the stupid husband that Mary was really a little lamb with fleece as white as snow ? I think yes, but Sir Patrick Hastings pretends to think no.

All this because Mary's husband, when he came out of prison, went off to Africa, where he heard of a riverful of diamonds ; and also because one of the most effective of theatrical gestures is for the hero to throw a queen's ransom or its equivalent at the feet of the woman he despises. (See Armand Duval's point-blank discharge of wads of banknotes at the humiliated Marguerite.) Strangely enough, on her inevitable way out to the West Coast of Africa Mary met a young gentleman who also believed that the only way to her heart lay through the tiara ; so both husband and honourable lover went off to find the river, leaving Mary and a chaperon to mark time for twelve months in the salubrious watering-places round Lagos. Very respectfully I suggest to Sir Patrick that his case for the diamond hunters is too thin. The best excuse for diamond-hunting is that the stones are jolly things to look for, and jolly valuable things when you have found them. But to risk your own life and your friend's limb, and a charge of cowardice when, in order to get the diamonds to the coast, you have to leave the other fellow to be cut up by hostile natives—to risk all this out of sentiment for a woman who has given the clearest proof that she likes you rather less than anybody else on earth is the " commercial " theatre with a vengeance. In other words it is pure nonsense, and I should not be surprised if Sir Patrick knows it.

The second act, which showed Mr. Leslie Faber with a broken heart and Mr. Owen Nares with a broken leg, was real good fun. It was full of howling natives, of those " Portuguese and Greeks " of the sort immortalised by Mr. Tom Clare, of fights in the stockade *à la Masterman Ready.* It may be that Providence designed the continent of Africa to be something other than a setting for disputes between Sahibs as to the

ultimate ownership of a Memsahib belonging to one of
them, and I confess that it always strikes me as a little
unfair upon the native that he should not be expected
to behave as a man and a brother until the moment when
he realises that the Englishmen with the diamonds are
two in number, and that hundreds of his kind are to
be fobbed off with a yard of calico and half a dozen
beads. However, that is by the way. What is more
important is that Mr. Clifford Mollison, who as a
Cockney servant was the life and soul of the piece and
also its only death, secured an instantaneous and
immense success. The house rose at him, and it was
very naughty of Sir Patrick to kill him off.

The third act devolved into a long and tedious discussion as to whether Mr. Faber should have left Mr.
Nares in the lurch, if indeed he had done so, most people
on the stage arguing that he had shot him and made off
with the booty. All this was cleared up when just on
time Mr. Nares limped in, having walked some hundreds of miles in eight weeks with a broken leg. This
was characteristic of Mr. Nares's pluck, since in the
first act he set off for the Heart of Darkness at one
minute's notice and with absolutely no luggage. Mr.
Eric Stanley aired beneath the African canopy all the
sentiments which are proper to the bow-windows of
English clubland, and aired them well. There was
never any real hope of Miss Jessie Winter getting out
of her first entanglement with her ferocious husband.
So she patted Mr. Nares on the back and dismissed him
to the consolations of the bathroom and somebody

else's second-best toothbrush. Miss Helen Ferrers, Mr. William Hallman, and Mr. Lewin Mannering fitted in agreeably or disagreeably as their parts commanded.

*June* 2.

# "No. 17"

A Joyous Melodrama by JEFFERSON FARJEON

## New Theatre

ALL plays are too long. Mr. Shaw has been heard to express an opinion to the contrary, but I reiterate : all plays are too long. And this because they do not contain sufficient material. Mr. Shaw's Pentateuchs, biological and otherwise, are really only studies for a drama which it would take a good week to play. But the average West End comedy contains the sketch of an idea some half-hour long, which has then got to be stretched to such a length that ten shillings and sixpence may reasonably be demanded for it. Any play, therefore, of which the material is too thin must in performance play too long. Imagine the impatience of the dramatic critic who has to sit night after night through a three hours' exposition of what any competent dramatist—competent in the old-fashioned mid-Victorian sense—would have got through in forty minutes. Now it is utterly impossible for the dramatic critic to get away before the end of the piece. He has to wait and listen while the call-boy and the cloak-room attendant are being thanked for their extraordinary and unprecedented services in the cause of British Drama. This in case the theatre is burned down. And, therefore, since he may not cut the play short at the end, he can, and sometimes will, cut it short at the beginning.

Doubtless this is a very bad habit. Yet by pursuing it steadfastly I have so far escaped that ruination of the digestive organs which sours and embitters the life of every critic. Nothing conduces to cerebral lucidity more than a cup of coffee, a glass of old brandy, and a cigar. In some placidity, undisturbed by the magpie horde which on a first night simply will not get itself into its seat, but must hang about to see whether Lord X. is bringing Lady Y., and if not, why not—in some mood of reasonable receptivity, therefore, I have often slipped into my seat and instinctively deduced all that was essential in those first five unnecessary minutes. Now, a good play is one in which every word, every silence, and every lift of an eyebrow matters from the word " Go ! " I imagine that the playgoer who arrives too late for the ghost in *Hamlet* really would not make very much of the piece. A good play, therefore, is one of which you cannot afford to miss the first five minutes. I will swear that I was not more than five minutes late for the new piece at the New Theatre entitled *No.* 17. And since for the remaining three hours not one word of the entertainment was intelligible to me, or came within cometary distance of the understandable, I conclude that this play must have been a very good one indeed.

I am very sorry about those five minutes. When I arrived a merchant sailor was conducting a nice-looking young gentleman up a winding staircase which presently turned into an empty room on the floor of which lay a corpse fully furnished with handcuffs and revolver. I gathered that the sailor had been looking for a cheap night's lodging, and that the young man had been taking the air in a quiet Galsworthian way when the sailor ran downstairs to tell him about the corpse. And then things began to happen. The young man accused the sailor of murder, and instead of going for the police went off to explore the house. Whereupon the sailor, bored with the corpse, bundled it into the next room, whereupon it promptly took to its heels. Then the young man came back. The two then made the discovery of a secret door, upon which was a placard giving the prospectus of some kind of " International Crime Agency." A girl in distress then appeared through a skylight. Then the door rattled and there appeared the heroine, accompanied by the most villainous uncle modern history affords, and a tall dark fellow with the manner of a commercial traveller, who was apparently a total stranger to both of them, and yet allied by the closest ties known to criminal record. About this period the act drop fell.

For some reason, understood possibly of the people on the stage, but entirely incomprehensible to me, it was found necessary to tie the nice young man and the distressed girl into a couple of chairs. Having done this, the villainous uncle produced a knuckle-duster and threatened to knock the nice young man's brains out. Reflecting, with Macbeth, that when the brains are out the man will die, one hoped for a quick and happy release for all parties concerned, including the audience. But it was not to be, for the heroine said she would stand for a lot of things, but not for murder. So the three people more obviously labelled villains went out, presumably to take a little well-earned refreshment at a coffee-stall, it being about four o'clock in the morning. The nice young man then joggled himself on the chair as far as the secret cupboard, the lock whereof being turned there fell out the sailor and the corpse, the latter having slipped in whilst we were looking at something else. Now a young man with a stammer came in through a pane of glass. As he was a friend of the nice young man, and showed himself willing to untie him and the distressed young girl, there seemed no reason why all these nice people should not betake themselves to their homes and beds, leaving No. 17 and the three obvious villains to look after themselves.

But when the act drop went up again we found ourselves cheerfully assembled in the cellar. It was a remarkable cellar, decorated after the manner of a modern night club. The arras being drawn back, a sliding panel was revealed. This, being slid, disclosed a complicated system of clocks and levers. The right combination found by the villainous uncle, who, entering with heroine and commercial traveller, had, as a preliminary, bound and gagged all the nice people, a lever was pulled and the floorboards opened to disclose a yawning grave. Or, rather, a kind of grave. For we were told that the cellar was built over a tunnel on a railway line, and that it was the habit of the villain to tip his victims into the empty trucks of passing luggage trains. There was some talk of a diamond necklace, and the game appeared to be to find out who in the piece were detectives and who were thieves. The uncle was tipped into one passing train, while the stuttering young gentleman clambered out of another. Which ought to have made matters easier, but didn't. At the end I believed that the young man of Galsworthian aspect came from Scotland Yard, and that the stammering friend was his assistant. I believed also that the uncle and the commercial traveller were crooks. But who the corpse was and who the distressed young woman remained for me complete and entire mysteries. As for the sailor in the Merchant Service, he was obviously put in merely to make the whole thing more difficult. My complaint about this piece is simply that it didn't amuse me. I adore detective stories and mystery plays, but only on condition that the mystery is of a reasonable kind admitting of a reasonable solution. The whole fun of the thing consists in trying to discover the solution. But the proceedings at the New Theatre made no appeal to any kind of reason. If the whole company had stood on their heads and spoken their sentences backwards way about the confusion would have been in no whit increased. Let there be no misunderstanding. I enjoy plays like *Raffles* and *Bulldog Drummond* more almost than any other kind of plays. I adore any kind of mystery piece so long as it remains within the bounds of human reasoning, but I dislike intensely entertainments which have apparently been devised for lunatics. One of the most annoying things about this production was a piece of gorgeous acting by Mr. Leon M. Lion. It was annoying because one would have liked to see it in better surroundings. Anything richer in scope, fantasy and variety, anything more human and lovable, anything livelier or more truly droll than Mr. Lion's merchant seaman I never wish to see. Mr. Nicholas Hannen is in this piece. And over this bare fact this critic weeps.

*August* 19.

# " The Ghost Train "

A Melodrama by ARNOLD RIDLEY

St. Martin's Theatre

TO anybody with any zest for living there would
appear to be nothing to be said about old age
except that it is a lame and impotent conclusion. But
there are many things to be said against old age, and
amongst them is the fact that we grow to know too
much. A little learning is a dangerous thing, and
excess of knowledge can be a spoil-sport. Isn't it
Pierre Loti who sees in the *ennui* of Omniscience an
argument for an infinity of First Causes ? Loti is taking
his soul for an airing at two o'clock on a winter's morning in the heart of the Pyrenees, and apart from two
Customs officers not a mouse stirs. Gazing through
frosty space at Vega in the constellation of the Harp,
Loti falls to wondering whether smuggling is a matter
of first importance. That Vega is, so to speak, our
next-door neighbour opens up the question of multiple
Universes, each the lobby to the next, and this in turn
brings further speculation. " The Jehovah who should
be all—must I not be filled with pity for that timeless
vigil in awe, loneliness and absolute free will ? To

content that microscopic reason which is mine there must be an endless progression of Deities, so that always above that Power which we know, however mighty and however awful, must be one more yet more eternal and inaccessible." And Loti's night-piece ends in vertigo.

The philosopher who bade us hitch our wagon to a star said nothing about unhitching. The climb down from the Immensities is not easy, and I am afraid my pen has run away with me. Did we set out to discuss a play? We did. And did the play pretend to deal in the Unknown? Verily. And did it deceive us all and turn out in the middle of the third act not to be about the Unknown, but about such knowledgeable things as China clay and machine-guns? Yes. And did those of us who are old playgoers—to get back to our starting-point—did not the elderly know that disillusion must await them about 10.30? And was not their evening largely spoilt in consequence? Again, yes. It seems to me to be a stupid convention which postulates that plays setting a four-dimensional problem must find a three-dimensional solution. This rule does not obtain in the better kind of ghost stories, where a mystery is allowed to remain a mystery and a Ghost Ship flies a ghostly pennant to the end; and one does not see why plays should not have equal license. But the theatre is a strange place. Let the piece move on the plain of the perfectly matter-of-fact, and the solution will be in terms of the wildest unreason —one might instance that drama in which a pearl-thief tears up a dubious cheque for ten thousand pounds so that she may fall on the bosom of the young man to whose advances she has previously preferred three years in gaol. Monstrous concatenation ! But let the play begin in some unexplored borderland, and inevitably its conclusion must be more prosaic than Clapham Junction.

*The Ghost Train* began well enough. The curtain drew up and exhibited one of those waiting-rooms in country railway stations to kick one's heels in which is to have a ghastly foretaste of eternity. It is the dead of a foggy night, and the stationmaster by lighting the gas gives Melancholy a substance and a shape. A train, hardly glimpsed through the frost and filth of the window-panes, comes into the station and departs. (This is surely one of the best sound-effects ever compassed on any stage.) And then a number of passengers enter. They have missed their connection, and must spend the night in the waiting-room many miles from anywhere. But the stationmaster will not let them doss down, since it is against the Bye-laws. They reason, but he is adamant. They show him money and he becomes less adamant, until at the sight of more money he is no longer adamant at all. But now he tells them some story of a hideous railway accident which happened on that very night twenty-one years ago, and how, every Tenth of November, as it strikes midnight, the Ghost Train rushes through the station, accompanied by flopping corpses and other hideous phenomena. It is the Tenth of November, and the passengers have an hour in which to get clear and save their nervous systems. But it is the passengers' turn to be stubborn, and most stubborn of all is the silly ass by whose fault the connection was missed in the beginning. So the passengers hold firm, the station-master departs, and midnight comes after much bracing and some failure of the spirit.

With midnight duly arrives the Ghost Train. Invisible faces peer in at the window, and we realise that though seen faces may be vile, unseen faces are villainy itself. A crimson light creeps along the bottom moulding of the window-pane, as it were the red hair of some ghostly marauder. Nothing has been omitted which could conceivably add to our mental and moral discomfort, not even that old tag about there being more things in heaven and earth, etc., etc. Could anything be better ? one asks. Why, then, not send us home scared out of our wits ? Why not show the effect of ghostly apparition upon a man who is convinced that he has seen a ghost ? There is a good deal to be said for the theory that anybody who really believed in the supernatural must go out of his mind, and that he who can tell with calmness the story of ghostly visitation does not really credit it. But again my pen is straying. What I am striving to indicate is that the end of this play is footle, and that the elderly among us knew all along that it could only be footle.

The piece was very well acted. Mr. Caleb Porter really did convey some suggestion of the eerie, although he turned out to be as big a deceiver as anybody else.

Mr. Frederick Cooper gave nonchalance its utmost value, though one would deem it a mistake always to cast this clever actor for absurdity. Miss Gladys Ffolliott provided for a time her usual extremely amusing relief of acerbity, but to our infinite regret was sent into a sleep of intoxication early on in the play. This was a lamentable piece of judgment, very much as if Shakespeare had got frightened by Falstaff after the first scene and consigned him to after-dinner torpor. It should be said that Miss Mary Clare made an appearance *en chair et en os*. There is very little that is ghost-like about this extremely talented actress except the tenuity of the parts to which she has been recently condemned. Miss Clare is indeed unfortunate. Either she is given something unworthy of her skill, or she has a rattling good part in a play which nobody dreams of visiting.

*November 23.*

# " The Shame Woman "

## A Melodrama by Lulu Vollmer

### Elephant and Castle Theatre

ONE of the most interesting things about this performance was the house, which was packed from floor to ceiling. For rather more than twelve months the management of this theatre has run a stock company which each week has chosen and performed a piece out of its repertory for the delight of its many patrons. The point to be made here is that the audience exercises patronage in the full sense of the word, since it is composed of individuals who go regularly and often. The patrons are many, and there has been no doubt about their delight. Add that other theatre not so very many stone's-throws away, and one realises the fact that on the south side of the river the repertory system is an immense success. Is there a reproach here to playgoers on the more fashionable side ? Yes. It is not an adequate defence to pretend that the Elephant Theatre has been devoted to the tawdriest kind of melodrama and the " Old Vic " to a standard implacably high. The truth is that there are not enough educated playgoers in the heart of the West End with sufficient

persistence and enthusiasm to keep going any kind of
theatre with any kind of repertory.

The plays which have successfully prevailed over
the water have not depended for their drawing power
upon a fashionable cast, expensive dressing and mount-
ing, or even novelty of subject. They have belonged
to that order which by virtue of its great age remains
for ever new, the crudeness of whose examples does not
obscure the fact that melodrama is tragedy which has
passed through the mesh of a common mind. There
is nothing in the plot of *The Shame Woman* which would
have prevented Shakespeare from using it as the theme
for a big play, which is more than can be said for ninety-
nine out of every hundred pieces produced in the West
End. Indeed, one scene in which a baleful harridan
and village midwife steals meat and bread from the
cupboard of a client, and, keeping the richer portion for
herself, fobs off with the merest crumb her fork'd radish
of a husband—this scene had plenty of tang and gusto,
and could without the alteration of a word have gone
straight into an Elizabethan comedy. The play might
take for its motto the sixth line in the sixty-sixth sonnet ;
and it is not to be condemned because the maiden virtue
which is strumpeted dwells in North Carolina. There
were several very moving touches, as when the mother
first showed by the gift of baby-linen her knowledge of
her daughter's misfortune, and again when the girl
fell to a curious inspection of the tiny gown. The first
half of the play was made up of incidents which were
admirable in exact measure as they were foreseen ; it

was only when modern introspection got to work that it became less good. Only a perverted imagination, one thinks, would pretend that a woman is justified in going to the scaffold to save the reputation of another who is already dead. This savours too much of " what the neighbours think," and it is at this point that tragedy passes through the melodramatic sieve. The first half of the play, then, has a certain accustomed grip ; the second half left one with the feeling that they do these things more convincingly in the cinema.

The acting suffered throughout from one great fault—its appalling slowness. Every character uttered each and every word as though it were an isolated adventure in speech. A sentence was like a succession of stones dropped into a well, and a harangue became an archipelago of silence thinly dotted with interruptions. But the audience did not seem to mind this, and perhaps a capacity for steady attention should be rated as highly as mere quickness of apprehension. At the end of the play and after the heroine had disappeared for execution the curtain did not fall. Instead the orchestra struck up a lively tune and the characters filed across the stage in single procession, beginning with the meanest and working up to the most magnanimous. The applause was equally divided, as who should say that in melo-drama nobody can do more than his bit. Let me not, therefore, make distinction among the many who did their bits so well.

*November* 26.

# Index

Abbas, Marta, 50.
Achurch, Janet, 27.
Ainley, Henry, 166, 244.
Albanesi, Eva, 67.
Allanby, Frank, 180.
Allgood, Sara, 117.
*And That's the Truth*, 55–59.
*Antony and Cleopatra*, 27–30.
*Anyhouse*, 204–208.
*Ariadne, or Business First*, 134–139.
Arundale, Sybil, 76.
Atkins, Robert, 21.
Ault, Marie, 42, 113.
Aylmer, Felix, 254, 277.
Aynesworth, Allan, 139, 197.

Baddeley, Angela, 26, 76.
Baddeley, Hermione, 264.
Bancroft, George, 234.
Bannerman, Margaret, 185, 189.
Bankhead, Tallulah, 133, 139.
Banks, Leslie, 171, 218, 254.
Barnard, Ivor, 112, 208.
Barrymore, John, 12, 15.
Barton, Mary, 239.
Bateman, Leah, 35, 113.
Batley, Dorothy, 248.
Benham, Ernest, 248.
Best, Edna, 139, 142.
Birch, Frank, 113.
Bird, Richard, 223.
Blakelock, Denys, 142.
Bond, Charles, 35.
Booth, Edwin, 19.
Burbidge, Douglas, 214.
Byrne, Cecily, 142.

Cadell, Jean, 192.
*Cæsar and Cleopatra*, 224–228.
Caine, Henry, 122.
*Camilla States Her Case*, 182–185.
Camp, Shep, 162.
Carson, Charles, 41.
Carten, Audrey, 171.
Carter, Margaret, 109, 171.
Casson, Lewis, 7, 26, 112, 122.
*Caste*, 215–219.
*Cherry Orchard, The*, 77–82.
Clare, Mary, 255, 293.
Clarence, O. B., 81.
Clark, Holman, 222.
Clarkson, Willie, 66.
Claughton, Susan, 239.
Codrington, Ann, 239.
Collier, Constance, 15.
Compton, Fay, 15, 16, 139.
Cooper, Frederick, 15, 293.
Cooper, Gladys, 96, 147, 243.
Cowie, Laura, 41.
*Cristilinda*, 194–198.
Curzon, George, 277.

Dawson, Ivo, 180.
Denham, Reginald, 63, 67, 167.
Deverell, John, 139.
Doble, Frances, 93.
*Doctor Faustus, The Tragical History of*, 31–36.
*Doll's House, A*, 68–72.

*L'École des Cocottes*, 94–97.
Elsom, Isobel, 196, 271.
Elton, George, 166.

# Index

Evans, Edith, 20, 21, 28, 29.
Evans, Gwendolen, 81.

Faber, Leslie, 97, 280.
*Fallen Angels*, 134–139.
Farebrother, Violet, 189, 219.
Ferrars, Helen, 282.
Ffolliott, Gladys, 293.
Ffrangçon-Davies, Gwen, 108, 228.
Field, Alexander, 35.
Field, Ben, 15, 254.
Filmer, A. E., 109.
Franklin, A. E., 66.
Freeman, Frank, 198.

Gardener, Shayle, 15.
Garside, 21.
*Ghost Train, The*, 289–293.
Gielgud, 35, 81, 87, 97.
*Gloriana*, 124–128.
*Godless, The*, 89–93.
Gott, Barbara, 162.
Green, Dorothy, 59, 214.
*Green Hat, The*, 129–133.
Greet, Clare, 67, 122.
Gregory, Dora, 208.
Grey, Mary, 81.
Grisewood, H., 66, 189.

Haddon, Peter, 223.
Hambling, Arthur, 123.
*Hamlet*, 11–16.
Hammond, Aubrey, 109.
Hamilton, Diana, 175.
Hannen, Nicholas, 6, 239, 288.
Hardwicke, Cedric, 41, 228.
Harris, Clare, 165, 176.
Harris, Robert, 113, 255.
*Hay Fever*, 149–156.
Hay, John Le, 109.
Haye, Helen, 202.
Hayes, George, 112.
Hayes, Patricia, 42.
Heatherley, Clifford, 202.
Heatherley, Lois, 239.
*Henry IV.*, 48–55.
*Henry VIII.*, 22–26.

Hignett, H. R., 35.
Hilliard, Stafford, 239.
Hollman, William, 282.
Holloway, Baliol, 18, 21, 29.
Hudd, Walter, 208.
Hunt, Martita, 72.
Hunter, Ian, 142, 254.
Hutchinson, Harry, 118.

Isham, Gyles, 66.
Isham, Virginia, 81.
*Iris*, 240–244.
Ivor, Frances, 238.

Jackson, Florence, 233.
James, J. H., 66.
Jeans, Isabel, 212.
Jeayes, Allan, 176, 239.
Jeffreys, Ellis, 148.
Jensen, Christine, 239.
Jerrold, Mary, 192.
Jones, Robert Edmund, 15.
*Juno and the Paycock.* 114–118.

Kean, Edmund, 20.
Keen, Malcolm, 15, 160.
Keith-Johnston, Colin, 112.
Kendall, Henry, 223.
Kerr, Mollie, 254.
King, Ada, 26, 123.
*Kismet*, 250–255.

Lawton, Frank, 148.
Lanchester, Elsa, 36
Landi, Elissa, 193, 255.
Lang, Matheson, 270.
Lathbury, Stanley, 108, 228.
*Last of Mrs. Cheyney, The*, 144–148.
*Lavender Ladies*, 190–193.
Leahy, Eugene, 7.
Lefeuvre, Guy, 59, 214.
Leister, Frederick, 133.
Lindo, Olga, 161, 203.
Lion, Leon M., 92, 288.
Lister, Frances, 203.
Livesey, Sam, 128, 255.
Lloyd, Frederick, 72.

Loder, Basil, 148, 171.
Lowne, C. M., 185.
*Lullaby*, 186–189.
Lytton, Doris, 239.

*Madras House, The*, 235–239.
Mannering, Lewin, 282.
Marford, Charles, 21.
Marshall, Herbert, 192.
Massey, Raymond, 122.
Matcham, Eliot, 123.
Mather, Aubrey, 97, 219, 254.
Maturin, Eric, 133.
Maud, J., 66.
Maude, Joan, 67.
Maurier, Sir Gerald du, 147.
McKinnel, Norman, 133.
Milton, Ernest, 54.
Milward, Dawson, 148.
Mollison, Clifford, 218.
*Moon and Sixpence, The*, 163–167.
Moore, Hilda, 171, 208.
Morgan, Sydney, 118.
*Mrs. Warren's Profession*, 229, 234.

Napier, Alan, 81.
Nares, Owen, 280.
Nesbit, Tom, 208.
Nesbitt, Cathleen, 142.
Ney, Marie, 239.
*No. 17*, 283–288.
Norman, Norman V., 25.
Novello, Ivor, 248.
Nye, L., 66.

Oates, Cicely, 176.
O'Brien, Terence, 41.
O'Donovan, 81.
*Old Heidelberg*, 245–249.
*On 'Change*, 220–223.
O'Neil, Peggy, 201.
O'Neill, Norman, 198.
Onslow, Alexander, 248.
*Ordeal*, 272–277.
Oughton, Winifred, 122, 239.
*Overture*, 172–176.

*Peer Gynt*, 60–67.
Percy, Esme, 41.
Playfair, Nigel, 59, 212.
Porter, Caleb, 292.
Porter, Neil, 21, 29, 35.
Price, Nancy, 59, 128, 175.
*Prisoners of War, The*, 110–113.
Pusey, Arthur, 202, 219.

Quong, Rose, 42.

*Rain*, 157–162.
Rains, Claude, 59, 213, 238.
Rawson, Tristan, 128, 171.
Reynolds, Tom, 166.
*Richard III.*, 17–21.
Richards, Valérie, 233.
Ricketts, Charles, 26.
*Rivals, The*, 211–214.
*River, The*, 278–282.
Roberts, J. H., 93, 160.
Rosmer, Milton, 72, 75.
Rooke, Irene, 238.
Rorke, Mary, 185.
*Round Table, The*, 119–123.
Royce, Julian, 133.
Ruggeri, Ruggero, 50.

Sage, Stuart, 162.
Saunders, Florence, 36.
Scott-Gatty, 171, 189.
*Sea-Gull, The*, 83–88.
*Sea Urchin, The*, 199–203.
Seyler, Athene, 180.
Seymour, Madeleine, 277.
Sewell, Charles, 233.
*Shame Woman, The*, 194–196.
Sharp, Eileen, 166.
Shaw, George Bernard, 22.
*Show, The*, 259–264.
Sinclair, Arthur, 117.
*Six Characters in Search of an Author*, 45–48.
Skillan, George, 42.
Sloane, Olive, 208.
Smith, Beatrice, 122.
Speaight, R. W., 66.
*Spring Cleaning*, 140–143.

# Index

Squire, Ronald, 142, 147.
Stanley, Eric, 281.
Stewart, Athole, 97.
Sunderland, Scott, 228.
Swallow, Margaret, 88.
*Swallow, The*, 168–171.
Swete, E. Lyall, 25.
Swinburne, Mercia, 219.
Swinburne, Nora, 203.
Swinley, Ion, 34, 35, 75, 108.

Tandy, A., 66.
*Tarnish*, 199–203.
Taylor, Valérie, 87.
Tempest, Marie, 156, 180.
*Tess of the D'Urbervilles*, 105–109.
Thesiger, Ernest, 35.
Thomas, Agnes, 239.
Thomas, E. W., 248.
Thomson, Beatrix, 218.
Thorndike, Sybil, 5, 6, 24, 25, 101, 122.
Thorpe, Courtenay, 15.
Titheradge, Madge, 68, 72.
*Torch Bearers, The*, 177–181.
Travers, Roy, 15.
Tree, Viola, 41.
Trever, Austin, 108.
*Tyrant, The*, 265–271.

Upton, Leonard, 133.

Vanne, Marda, 161.
Venne, Lottie, 223.
*Verge, The*, 98–101.

Walcott, Donald, 277.
Waring, Herbert, 15.
Watson, Margaret, 202.
Webster, Lizzie, 109.
Welsh, Jane, 277.
Whale, James, 80, 88.
*White Devil, The*, 37–42.
White, J. Fisher, 93.
Whitty, May, 148.
*Wild Duck, The*, 73–76.
Wilkinson, Norman, 16, 212.
Will, Ian O., 248.
Williams, Harcourt, 72.
Wills, Brember, 76.
Wills, Drusilla, 109.
Wilson, Beatrice, 35.
Wincott, Geoffrey, 55.
Winston, Bruce, 7, 26, 35.
Winter, Jessie, 281.
Wontner, Arthur, 35.
Wright, Haidée, 254, 277.

Yarde, Margaret, 166, 171.
Yarrow, Duncan, 21, 29.